MECHANICS 89

Capitalization 90

Abbreviations 94

DOCUMENTATION 99

MLA Style of Documentation 100

APA Style of Documentation 123

Chicago Style of Documentation 134

CBE Style of Documentation 139

GLOSSARY OF USAGE 145

INDEX 159

INTRODUCTION

The *Checkmate Pocket Guide* is a valuable reference tool for quickly finding answers to your writing style and grammar questions, with the bonus of a detailed section on documentation. Its pocket-size format makes this a truly portable handbook that fits easily into backpack or pocket.

Despite its compact size, *Checkmate* includes comprehensive coverage of grammar; general writing style; punctuation; writing mechanics such as capitalization, when and how to use abbreviations, and the proper use of italics; and documentation, based on the styles of the Modern Language Association, the American Psychological Association, *The Chicago Manual of Style*, and the Council of Biology Editors, now known as the Council of Science Editors. Sample pages from student research essays provide you with models for formatting title pages, text, notes, and bibliographies.

Inside the front cover, the book's table of contents is laid out very clearly and simply. The "Grammar" section includes easy-to-follow tips for handling sentence fragments, problems with pronouns, subject–verb agreement, adjectives and adverbs, problems with modifiers, shifts, mixed constructions, and parallelism. The "Style" section discusses wordiness, as well as diction and audience. You will find helpful information on proper use of the comma, semicolon, colon, apostrophe, quotation marks, and others in the "Punctuation" section. "Mechanics" covers capitalization, abbreviations, and italics.

The most widely used and popular styles of documentation are discussed next, with many examples provided. *Checkmate Pocket Guide* then concludes with a concise glossary of correct word usage—including many words that are commonly misused—and an index that makes it easy to pinpoint any particular topic in the guide. In addition, a list of classroom correction symbols is provided on the inside of the back cover. Note, however, that some instructors use their own correction codes.

The design is similar to the *Pocket Guide*'s sister publication, *Checkmate*. We have remained true to the book's inviting, useful, clear, and easy-to-navigate style. Many examples are provided and colour is used strategically, helping students to locate references quickly and easily.

Checkmate Pocket Guide is invaluable for anyone who wants a portable, quick-reference source, and provides the guidance needed for students to become self-reliant writers in college and university and beyond.

Joane Buckley

Checkmate

Pocket Guide

Joanne Buckley

Australia Canada Mexico Singapore Spain United Kingdom United States

Checkmate Pocket Guide

by Joanne Buckley

Associate Vice-President, Editorial Director:
Evelyn Veitch

Executive Editor:
Rod Banister

Marketing Manager:
Lisa Rahn

Senior Developmental Editor:
Katherine Goodes

Senior Production Editor:
Natalia Denesiuk

Copy Editor:
June Trusty

Proofreader:
Rodney Rawlings

Indexer:
Edwin Durbin

Production Coordinator:
Ferial Suleman

Creative Director:
Angela Cluer

Interior Design:
Katherine Strain

Interior Design Modificatio
Tammy Gay

Cover Design:
Peter Papayanakis

Cover Images:
top: Ayumi Moriuchi/Photonica
bottom: Gary Buss/Taxi/Gett Images

Compositor:
Tammy Gay

Printer:
Transcontinental

Printed and bound in Canada
1 2 3 4 07 06 05 04

For more information contact Nelson, 1120 Birchmount Road, Toronto, Ontario, M1K 5G4. Or you can visit our Internet site at http://www.nelson.com

Library and Archives Canad Cataloguing in Publication Data

Buckley, Joanne, 1953–
Checkmate pocket guide / Joanne Buckley.

Includes index.
ISBN 0-17-641528-9

1. English language—Rhetoric. 2. English language—Grammar. I. Title.

PE1408.B8185 2004
808'.042
C2004-905225-X

GRAMMAR

GRAMMAR

The following sections catalogue a number of common errors made by writers in English. Use these sections to revise your work and to respond to questions and suggestions about your use of language. If you discover that you have a tendency to make any one of these errors with some frequency, review the relevant section carefully to internalize the information you find. Doing so will improve your sense of grammar for the next piece of writing you complete.

Sentence Fragments

A sentence is one complete independent clause that contains a subject and verb. A **sentence fragment,** on the other hand, is part of a sentence that is set off as if it were a whole sentence: it starts with a capital letter and ends with a final period or other end punctuation. However, the fragment lacks essential requirements of a grammatically complete and correct sentence. The fragment may, for example,

1. lack a verb

   Just Phil and I.

2. lack a subject

   Pacing the hallway.

3. be a subordinate clause commencing with a subordinating word

   When I fly a kite.

Sentence fragments give readers a fragment of a thought as opposed to a complete thought, and they interfere with writing clarity. In any type of academic writing, sentence fragments are considered a serious writing error, and they must be eliminated.

TESTING FOR SENTENCE FRAGMENTS

Fragments can be spotted easily when they appear in isolation, but fragments are more difficult to identify when they are near complete sentences. If you suspect a group of words is a sentence fragment, consider the following:

- Does the word group have a verb?
  - ❑ YES. Consider the next question.
  - ❑ NO. *The word group is a fragment and must be revised to include a verb.*

- Does the word group have a subject?
  - ❑ YES. Consider the next question.
  - ❑ NO. *The word group is a fragment and must be revised to include a subject.*
- Does the word group start with a subordinating word, making it a subordinate clause?
  - ❑ YES. *The word group is a sentence fragment and must be revised to create a complete sentence that is an independent clause.*
  - ❑ NO. If you answered yes to the two previous questions and no to this one, the word group is a complete sentence and does not require revision for sentence completeness.

Make sure to consider all three questions when reviewing your sentence, since a fragment could be missing more than one essential sentence element. If your evaluation indicates that you have a sentence fragment, use the following strategies to transform it into a complete sentence.

ELIMINATING SENTENCE FRAGMENTS

To fix the sentence fragment and make it a complete sentence, do one of the following:

1. Attach the sentence fragments to an independent clause, or a clause that contains the essential element lacking in the fragment (e.g., a subject or a verb).

   Just Phil and I were pacing the hallway.

2. Compose an independent clause from the fragment.

   At the emergency ward, the parents were pacing the hallway.

3. Drop the subordinating word.

   ~~When~~ I fly a kite.

SUBORDINATE CLAUSES

A subordinate clause contains a subject and a predicate, or verb, but the clause begins with a subordinating word or phrase, such as *after, although, if,* or *until*, or a relative pronoun, such as *that, which, what, who*. Therefore, the clause is not independent.

You can make a subordinate clause into an independent clause in one of two ways:

1. Merge the subordinate clause with a nearby sentence.

   Many of Elmore Leonard's novels have been made into movies. Because he is an amazingly popular crime writer.

2. Delete the subordinating element of the clause.

   Many of Elmore Leonard's novels have been made into movies. Because he is an amazingly popular crime writer.

PHRASES

A phrase is a group of words that does not have either a subject or a verb and therefore cannot stand alone as an independent clause or sentence. Look at these examples:

to go kayaking

for the umpteenth time

with great trepidation

Major types of phrases include noun phrases, adjective phrases, adverb phrases, and prepositional phrases.

FIXING PHRASE FRAGMENTS

You can address phrase fragment problems in two ways:

1. Incorporate the phrase into a nearby sentence.

   Our community library has an amazing array of resources. For every local citizen to use.

   As a subscriber to the paranormal, he took part in the smudging. A ceremony using smoke to purify the psychic energy field, or aura, around a person.

2. Turn the phrase into a complete sentence by adding a subject, predicate (verb), or both.

   Smokejumpers land with heavy gear, including two parachutes, puncture-proof Kevlar suits, freeze-dried food, fire shelters, and personal effects. cardboard boxes heaved out of the airplane are chain saws, shovels, and axes.

OTHER WORD GROUPS

Other commonly fragmented word groups include

- compound predicates
- examples introduced by *for example*, *such as*, and *for instance*
- lists

The following section will help you identify these fragmentation problems and provides strategies for correcting them.

COMPOUND PREDICATES

The predicate is the part of the sentence that contains the verb. It indicates what the subject is doing or experiencing, or what is being done to the subject. A **compound predicate** contains two or more predicates with the same subject.

> Joel wanted to buy a new computer and printer~~. But~~ but could afford to purchase only a used laptop.

EXAMPLES INTRODUCED BY **FOR EXAMPLE, SUCH AS,** *AND* **FOR INSTANCE**

Often you will need to introduce examples, illustrations, and explanations to support arguments and ideas in your academic writing. Some common words and phrases used to introduce examples, illustrations, and explanations include the following:

> *also, and, as an illustration, besides, but, equally important, especially, for example, for instance, furthermore, in addition, in particular, including, like, mainly, namely, or, specifically, such as, that is, to illustrate*

Sometimes a fragment introduced by any one of the above words or phrases can be attached to the sentence before it to create a complete sentence.

> Any treatment of early-seventeenth-century English literature must include a discussion of the period's leading figures~~. Such~~ , such as John Donne, Ben Jonson, and John Milton.

However, in some instances you may find it necessary to change the fragment containing examples into a new sentence.

> Jan Morris's travel pieces cover many interesting cities~~. For~~ ; for instance, she ~~exploring~~ explores Beirut, ~~visiting~~ visits Chicago, and ~~discovering~~ discovers "The Navel City" of Cuzco.

FRAGMENTS IN LISTS

Occasionally, list elements are fragmented. This type of writing problem usually can be corrected by using a colon or dash.

> During my rare vacations, I work on my three R's. Reading, rest, and running.

ACCEPTABLE FRAGMENTS

Professional writers may use sentence fragments intentionally for emphasis or effect.

> *Creating Emphasis*
>
> A strange place it was, that place where the world began. A place of incredible happenings, splendours and revelations, despairs like multitudinous pits of isolated hells. A place of shadow-spookiness, inhabited by the unknowable dead. A place of jubilation and of mourning, horrible and beautiful.
>
> —*Margaret Laurence, "Where the World Began"*
>
> *Forming Transitions*
>
> Now for the con side.
>
> *Making Exclamations*
>
> Not bloody likely!
>
> *Answering Questions*
>
> And should we go along with this position? Under no circumstances.
>
> *Advertising*
>
> Proven effective.

Many instructors do not accept sentence fragments, even intentional ones, in formal writing. Fragments may be acceptable in less formal writing contexts, such as an informal personal essay or an article for a campus newspaper. Even in contexts where they are permitted, do not over-use sentence fragments.

Comma Splices and Fused Sentences

Incorrectly joining two or more independent clauses within a sentence is a writing error. An independent clause, or main clause, contains at least a subject and a verb, and the clause can stand on its own as a separate grammatical unit. When two independent clauses appear in a single sentence, they must be joined in one of two ways:

1. using a comma and one of the seven coordinating conjunctions: *and, but, for, nor, or, so, yet*
2. with a semicolon or other acceptable punctuation such as a dash or a colon

Fused sentences (also known as run-on sentences) or **comma splices** occur when two independent clauses are incorrectly joined within the same sentence.

FUSED SENTENCES

In a fused sentence, no punctuation or coordinating conjunction appears between the two independent clauses.

independent clause independent clause
[Canada's most famous ship is the Bluenose] [it was originally designed to fish and race.]

COMMA SPLICES

In comma splices, the independent clauses are joined (or spliced) with commas and no coordinating conjunction.

Canada's most famous ship is the *Bluenose*, it was originally designed to fish and race.

Writers often use conjunctive adverbs in place of coordinating conjunctions and, in so doing, create comma splice errors. A coordinating conjunction is one of these seven words: *and*, *but*, *or*, *nor*, *for*, *so*, and *yet*. A conjunctive adverb, on the other hand, is a word such as *furthermore*, *however*, or *moreover*. However, merely placing the word *however* and commas between two independent clauses does not correct a comma splice error.

Comma Splice Involving Conjunctive Adverb
Incorrect: Canada's most famous ship is the *Bluenose*, however, it was originally designed to fish and race.

IDENTIFYING FUSED SENTENCES OR COMMA SPLICES IN YOUR WRITING

Use the following checklist to determine if a sentence is fused or is a comma splice.

- The sentence contains two independent clauses.
  - ❑ NO. Neither of the errors applies.
  - ❑ YES. *Proceed to the next question.*
- The independent clauses are joined by a comma and a coordinating conjunction.
  - ❑ YES. The clauses are correctly joined.
  - ❑ NO. *Proceed to the next question.*

- The independent clauses are joined by a semicolon or other acceptable punctuation, such as a colon or a dash.
  - ❑ YES. The clauses are correctly joined.
  - ❑ NO. *Use one of the revision strategies provided in the next section to correct the fused sentence or comma splice.*

STRATEGIES FOR CORRECTING FUSED SENTENCES OR COMMA SPLICES

You have four major options for correcting fused sentences or comma splices:

1. Add a comma and a coordinating conjunction: *and, but, for, nor, or, so, yet.*

   Canada's most famous ship is the *Bluenose*, yet it was originally designed to fish and race.

2. Add a semicolon or other appropriate punctuation, such as a colon or a dash.

   Canada's most famous ship is the *Bluenose*; it was originally designed to fish and race.

   OR

   Canada's most famous ship is the *Bluenose*; however, it was originally designed to fish and race.

3. Revise the sentence to subordinate one of the clauses.

   Even though Canada's most famous ship is the *Bluenose*, it was originally designed to fish and race.

4. Turn each independent clause into a separate complete sentence.

   Canada's most famous ship is the *Bluenose*. It was originally designed to fish and race.

REVISION WITH COORDINATING CONJUNCTION

A comma must precede the coordinating conjunction: *and, but, for, nor, or, so, yet.*

It was –30°C with a wind-chill factor I still had to walk my dogs.

Mordecai Richler was a fine novelist, he was also an amusing essayist.

REVISION WITH SEMICOLON OR COLON

Use a semicolon without a conjunction if the relationship between the two independent clauses is very clear.

> The results of the chemistry experiment were disappointing; our attempt to turn salad dressing into fine cognac had failed miserably.

Use a semicolon and a comma with independent clauses that are joined with a conjunctive adverb or transitional phrase, such as

> *also, as a result, besides, consequently, conversely, for example, for instance, furthermore, in addition, in fact, meanwhile, moreover, nonetheless, next, on the other hand, otherwise, similarly, subsequently, then, therefore, thus*

> Margaret Atwood is Canada's foremost living novelist; furthermore, she is among our leading poets.

Use a colon if the first independent clause introduces the second.

> The requests are thorough and varied: a chicken or rabbit will be skinned, boned, quartered, shredded, turned into patties, prepared for stew, the liver for this, the kidney for that.

REVISION BY SEPARATING SENTENCES

This option for correcting fused sentence and comma splices is usually the most effective since it provides the most revision choices.

You will first need to decide which of the independent clauses you would like to emphasize.

> ~~The~~ When the family visited Niagara Falls, we enjoyed visiting the wax museum, playing mini-golf, and taking pictures of the falls.

> The rules of hockey developed in the 1870s~~, they~~ stipulated that there be nine players on a team instead of six as there are today.

> ~~There~~ Since there is a smog alert in south-central Ontario, people with breathing difficulties are not supposed to go outside.

REVISION BY RESTRUCTURING

Since the clauses in fused sentences and comma splices are independent, they can stand on their own as separate grammatical units.

> Those who run for office are required to give a speech~~, the~~ *. These* speeches must be no longer than five minutes in length.

> There is one council member from each region ~~the~~ *. The* chairperson is elected by the council members.

Problems with Pronouns

A pronoun is a word that replaces a noun or another pronoun. Three major types of pronoun problems occur frequently in writing:

1. antecedent agreement problems
2. reference problems
3. case problems:
   a) personal pronouns
   b) whether to use *who* or *whom* in sentences

PRONOUN–ANTECEDENT AGREEMENT

The antecedent is the word the pronoun replaces. If the antecedent is singular, the pronoun that refers to it must also be singular.

> The microbiologist adjusted his microscope.

Similarly, if the antecedent is plural, the pronoun must be plural.

> The choir members opened their song books.

Indefinite pronouns do not refer to any specific person, thing, or idea:

> *another, anybody, anyone, anything, each, either, everybody, everyone, everything, neither, nobody, none, no one, nothing, one, somebody, someone, something*

In formal English, treat indefinite pronouns as singular even though they may seem to have plural meanings.

> Anyone who knows the answer should enter it using his or her [not *their*] keyboard.

CORRECTING INDEFINITE-PRONOUN AGREEMENT PROBLEMS

1. Change the plural pronoun to a singular, such as *he or she*.

   When the airplane hit severe turbulence, everyone feared for
   his or her
   ~~their~~ safety.

2. Make the pronoun's antecedent plural.

   the passengers
   When the airplane hit severe turbulence, ~~everyone~~ feared for their safety.

3. Recast the sentence to eliminate the pronoun agreement problem.

   safety was a common fear
   among all those on board
   When the airplane hit severe turbulence, ~~everyone feared for their safety~~.

Since the use of *his or her* can be awkward and wordy, especially if used repeatedly, you might consider correction strategies 2 and 3 as preferable alternatives.

GENERIC NOUNS

A **generic noun** names a typical member of a group, such as a typical *classroom teacher*, or a typical *dentist*. Generic nouns might appear to be plural; however, they are singular, and any pronouns referring to them must also be singular.

Each Olympic athlete must sacrifice if he or she *plans* [not *they plan*] to win a gold medal.

COLLECTIVE NOUNS

A collective noun names a group of people or things. Examples of collective nouns include the following words:

audience, army, choir, class, committee, couple, crowd, faculty, family, group, jury, majority, number, pack, team

If the Collective Noun Refers to a Unit

Use the singular pronoun.

The audience stood and applauded to show its approval.

If Parts of the Collective Noun Act Individually

Use a plural pronoun.

The audience folded their collapsible chairs and placed the seats in a storage room.

Often it is a good idea to emphasize that the antecedent is plural by adding a word, such as *members*, describing individuals within the group.

> The audience members folded their collapsible chairs and placed the seats in a storage room.

MAINTAIN SINGULAR OR PLURAL CONSISTENCY

Whether you treat the collective noun as singular or plural, ensure that you consistently treat references within the sentence as singular or plural, respectively.

> The faculty ~~have~~ has completed its review of courses for the upcoming term.

COMPOUND ANTECEDENTS

TWO OR MORE ANTECEDENTS JOINED BY **AND**

Antecedents joined by *and* form a **compound antecedent** and require a plural pronoun whether the antecedents are plural or singular.

> Dave and Michaela were starving after their [not *his and her*] day of skiing in Whistler.

TWO OR MORE ANTECEDENTS CONNECTED BY **OR, NOR, *EITHER . . . OR, NEITHER . . . NOR***

Make the pronoun agree with the nearest antecedent.

> Either Melodie or the Chans will have their way.

Note: With a compound antecedent such as the one above, place the plural noun last to prevent the sentence from sounding awkward.

> Neither the captain nor the other players could explain their lopsided defeat.

PRONOUN REFERENCE

A pronoun is a word that replaces a noun or another pronoun. Using pronouns allows you to avoid repeating nouns in speech and writing.

> Once Jarod made the sandwich, he packed it in a brown bag.

However, when the relationship between the antecedent and the pronoun is ambiguous, implied, vague, or indefinite, your intended meaning becomes unclear and may be completely lost to the reader.

AVOIDING AMBIGUITY ABOUT PRONOUN REFERENCE

When it is possible for a pronoun to refer to either one of two antecedents, the sentence is ambiguous.

Ambiguous: Franz told his father that his car needed a new transmission.

To eliminate the ambiguity, either repeat the clarifying antecedent or rewrite the sentence.

Option 1: Franz told his father that his father's car needs a new transmission.

Option 2: Franz said to his father, "Dad, your car needs a new transmission."

AVOIDING IMPLIED ANTECEDENTS

The reader should be able to clearly understand the noun antecedent of any pronoun you use. This antecedent must be stated and not implied or merely suggested.

Before the raging fire spread too close to nearby farms, ~~they~~ the residents were ordered to leave their homes.

Make sure that antecedents refer to nouns present in, or near, the sentence.

In ~~Naomi Wolf's~~ *The Beauty Myth*, ~~she~~ Naomi Wolf explores the relationship between gender and work.

AVOIDING VAGUENESS THROUGH USE OF THE PRONOUN ANTECEDENTS **THIS, THAT, WHICH,** *AND* **IT**

Pronouns such as *this*, *that*, *which*, and *it* should refer clearly to a specific noun antecedent and not to large groups of words expressing ideas or situations.

The international figure skating organization agreed to a major overhaul of the judging process; however, ~~it~~ the change took time.

A spot forecast may state that a temperature range for a specific canyon in the forest will be between 25 and 30 degrees, the humidity between 12 and 14 percent, and the winds 15 kilometres an hour. ~~This interests~~ All of these data interest firefighters.

AVOIDING INDEFINITE USE OF **IT, THEY,** *OR* **YOU**

Do not use the pronoun *it* indefinitely; for example, "In this book [article, chapter, and so on] it says . . ."

> ~~In~~ Chapter 23 of the textbook ~~it~~ states that one of the most important factors in transforming Canadian culture was the change in immigration patterns.

Never use *they* without a definite antecedent.

> the director, screenwriter(s), and actors
>
> In a typical Hollywood movie, ~~they~~ manipulate the audience's emotions.

In formal writing, the use of *you* is acceptable when you are addressing the reader directly.

> If you do not want the beeper on, select OFF, and if you want it loud, select HIGH.

In formal writing, do not use *you* as an indefinite pronoun.

> one
>
> In ancient Greece ~~you~~ dropped a mussel shell into a certain jar to indicate that a defendant was guilty.

PRONOUN CASE (*I* vs. *ME*, etc.)

Case refers to the form a noun or pronoun takes according to the function of that noun or pronoun in a sentence. In English there are three cases:

1. The **subjective case** indicates that the pronoun functions as a subject or a subject complement.
2. The **objective case** indicates that the pronoun functions as the object of a preposition or a verb.
3. The **possessive case** indicates that the pronoun shows ownership.

PRONOUN CASES

SUBJECTIVE	OBJECTIVE	POSSESSIVE
I	me	my
we	us	our
you	you	your
she/he/it	her/him/it	her/his/its
they	them	their

USING THE SUBJECTIVE CASE
The subjective case (*I, we, you, she/he/it, they*) must be used when the pronoun functions as a subject or as a subject complement.

As a Subject
Tony and I *split* the cost of the video.

A subject complement is a noun or adjective that follows a linking verb and renames or describes the sentence subject. Since the use of pronouns in the subjective case sounds quite different from the way you might use pronouns in informal speech, subjective case pronouns as subject complements frequently cause writing difficulties.

As a Subject Complement
Correct: The students who did the most work are Ivan and she.

Incorrect: The students who did the most work are Ivan and her.

In all formal writing, ensure that you use the subjective pronoun case when the pronoun is part of the subjective complement.

The woman Anatole married is she.

If the construction sounds too unnatural, you may wish to recast the sentence.

She is the woman Anatole married.

USING THE OBJECTIVE CASE
Use an objective case pronoun (*me, us, you, her/him/it, them*) if the pronoun functions as

1. a direct object

   The instructor asked her to read the poem.

2. an indirect object

   The invigilator provided Sam, Duncan, and me with pencils.

3. the object of a preposition

   Just between you and me, the Russian's routine was superior.

USING PRONOUNS IN COMPOUND SUBJECTS AND OBJECTS
A compound subject or a **compound object** includes more than one pronoun.

Compound Subject

She and I went to the multiplex to see a movie.

Compound Object

The park proposal surprised her and me.

The fact that the subject or object is compound does not affect the case of the pronoun. However, a compound structure often causes a writer to confuse pronoun case.

To determine if you have selected the correct pronoun case, try mentally blocking out the compound structure except for the pronoun in question. Then decide if the pronoun case you have selected is correct.

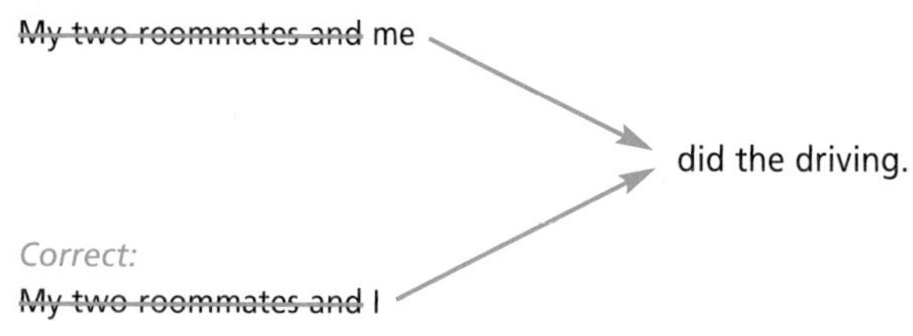

After the class, the librarian gave detentions to Rachel and ~~I~~ me.

In spite of our difficulties, my uncle and ~~me~~ I had a wonderful vacation in Mexico.

Avoid using a reflexive pronoun such as *myself* or *himself* when you are uncertain about the pronoun case.

The contest organizers sent the entry forms to Del and ~~myself~~ me.

USING PRONOUNS AS APPOSITIVES

An appositive is a noun or noun phrase that renames a noun, noun phrase, or pronoun. When a pronoun functions as an appositive, it has the same function, and hence case, as the noun or pronoun it renames.

Three members of the debating team—Clara, Michael, and ~~me~~ I—won a trophy.

Let's you and ~~I~~ me take the weekend off and go to the St. Jacob's market.

USING THE CORRECT PRONOUN CASE WHEN **WE** *OR* **US** *PRECEDES A NOUN*

Sometimes you may need to decide whether *we* or *us* should come before a noun or noun phrase. Mentally block out the noun so that only the pronoun remains. Then decide which pronoun case is correct.

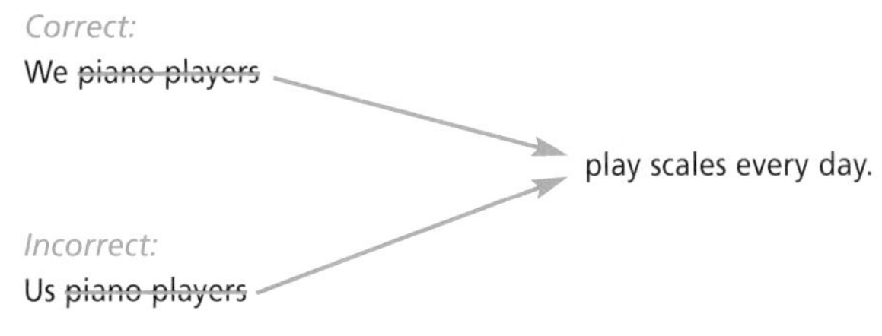

Follow the same procedure when considering pronouns that function as sentence objects.

The teacher yells at ~~we~~ us banjo players during every practice.

MAKING COMPARISONS USING **THAN** *OR* **AS** *WITH PRONOUNS*

When making comparisons using *than* or *as*, writers frequently leave out words because these words are clearly understood by readers.

Last year Bill Gates made more money than I ~~made money~~.

However, the case of the pronoun is determined by its function in the implied part of the sentence, which has been omitted. To determine the correct pronoun case in a sentence that uses *than* or *as* to make a comparison, supply the implied or missing part of the sentence. Then decide if the pronoun case is correct.

The groom is a full metre taller than ~~her~~ she is.

My late grandmother left my cousin as many family heirlooms as ~~I~~ me.

USING THE CORRECT PRONOUNS WITH INFINITIVES

The infinitive is the base (simple) form of a verb, usually following *to*, as in *to jump*. Both the subject and the object of an infinitive are in the objective case.

As the Subject of an Infinitive

The bride asked her [not *she*] to sing at the wedding.

As the Object of an Infinitive

Club members decided to elect him.

USING THE POSSESSIVE CASE TO MODIFY A GERUND

A **gerund** is a form of a verb that ends in *-ing* and is used as a noun; for example, *Fencing is my favourite sport*. Use a pronoun in the possessive case (*my, our, your, her/his/its, their*) to modify a gerund or gerund phrases.

> his
> The physical trainer disapproved of ~~him~~ *eating* bacon before workouts.

Nouns as well as pronouns can modify gerunds. The possessive is formed by adding an apostrophe and -s to the end of the noun.

> Wayne's *smoking* is the cause of his bad breath.

For more information on possessives, see pages 74–76.

WHO* AND *WHOM

Who and *whom* are pronouns. *Who* is the subjective case; it must be used only for subjects and subject complements. *Whom* is the objective case; it must be used only for objects.

1. *Who* and *whom* are used as interrogative pronouns to open questions.
2. As relative pronouns, *who* and *whom* are used to introduce subordinate clauses.

AS INTERROGATIVE PRONOUN TO OPEN QUESTIONS

To decide whether to use *who* or *whom*, you must first determine the pronoun's function within the question. Does the interrogative pronoun function as a subject or subject complement, or as an object?

> Who
> ~~Whom~~ commanded the coalition forces during the war in Afghanistan?

> Whom
> ~~Who~~ did the human resources manager interview?

AS RELATIVE PRONOUN TO INTRODUCE SUBORDINATE CLAUSES

Use *who* and *whoever* as relative pronouns for subjects and use *whom* and *whomever* for objects. When deciding which pronoun to use, you must determine whether the relative pronoun functions as a subject or object within the subordinate clause. A good technique to employ when making this decision is to mentally block off the main clause and focus on the subordinate clauses you are considering.

> The Nobel Prize for Literature is presented to ~~whomever~~ whoever has made the most significant contribution to literature over the course of a writing career.

> We don't know ~~who~~ whom the university president nominated to chair the committee.

Do not be misled by interrupting expressions such as *I know, they think,* or *she believes*, which often come after *who* or *whom* in a subordinate clause.

> The car dealer intends to invite only the customers ~~whom~~ who he thinks will want to attend.

Subject–Verb Agreement

Every sentence has a subject (stated or implied) and a verb. **Subject–verb agreement** refers to the relationship between the subject and the verb.

In the present tense, verbs must agree with subjects in two ways:

1. In **number**. Number means the subject can be singular (e.g., *I*) or plural (e.g., *we*).
2. In **person**. Person can be first person (*I, we*), second person (*you*), or third person (*she, he, it,* or *they*).

If the verb is a regular verb and the subject is in the third-person singular, use the -*s* (or -*es*) form of the verb.

> Tony *works* for his godfather.

PRESENT-TENSE FORMS OF *WORK*

	SINGULAR	PLURAL
FIRST PERSON	I *work*	we *work*
SECOND PERSON	you *work*	you *work*
THIRD PERSON	she/he/it *works*	they *work*

Notice how the following irregular verbs achieve subject–verb agreement.

PRESENT-TENSE FORMS OF *DO*	
I *do*	we *do*
you *do*	you *do*
she/he/it *does*	they *do*

PRESENT-TENSE FORMS OF *HAVE*	
I *have*	we *have*
you *have*	you *have*
she/he/it *has*	they *have*

The verb *to be* has different forms for the present and past tenses.

PRESENT-TENSE FORMS OF *BE*	
I *am*	we *are*
you *are*	you *are*
she/he/it *is*	they *are*

PAST-TENSE FORMS OF *BE*	
I *was*	we *were*
you *were*	you *were*
she/he/it *was*	they *were*

Often, if you have been speaking or writing English for a long time or know the language well, problems with subject–verb agreement will be obvious to your ear or eye. For example, the sentence *Jamie look good in his new tuxedo* immediately sounds or looks incorrect. It is obvious that the subject and verb do not agree. The sentence should be *Jamie looks good.*

However, some subject–verb agreement problems are more difficult to spot. A number of English sentence constructions make the subject difficult to identify—often the subject is located far from the verb—and, as a result, it is easy to make subject–verb agreement mistakes. Information in the following section will help you to avoid the most common subject–verb agreement problems.

WORDS BETWEEN SUBJECT AND VERB

Occasionally the modifying words between the sentence subject and verb include a noun, which might be mistaken for the subject. As a result, some writers use a verb that does not agree with the actual subject.

When evaluating any sentence for subject–verb agreement, mentally delete any modifying elements, such as prepositional phrases, so that only the sentence subject and verb remain. Then assess whether or not the subject and verb agree. You might consider drawing an arrow to connect the subject with the verb, as has been done in the following example.

The first ten minutes of a blind date *are* the most frightening.

The women in my residence ~~practises~~ practise kung fu for hours every day.

The course objective in both outlines ~~are~~ is to give the students enough rope to hang themselves if they do not complete the assignments on time.

Phrases beginning *along with, as well as, in addition,* and *together with* do not change the number of the subject because they are not part of the subject.

The prime minister, along with the cabinet, *was photographed* in the glamour shot.

SUBJECTS WITH *AND*

A compound subject contains two or more independent subjects joined by *and*. The compound subject requires a plural verb.

Tina and Mauri were inseparable.

The American Bulldog's unforgettable face and amazing athletic ability ~~has~~ have helped to make Harley a star of advertising media.

However, when the parts of the subject refer to a single person or idea, they require a singular verb.

Rice and tomato *is* a San Francisco treat.

Spaghetti and clam sauce *has* been a favourite in our house for years.

The pronouns *every* and *each* are singular, and require singular verbs, even if the subjects they precede are joined by *and*.

Every woman and man has a right to vote.

SUBJECTS WITH *OR* OR *NOR*

When a compound subject is joined by *or* or *nor*, make the verb agree with the part of the subject nearer to the verb.

Neither the tour guide nor his passengers *know* if the CN Tower is the world's tallest building.

Either the Beatles or Elvis Presley *has* had the most gold albums.

If my cousin or my aunts ~~is~~ are available, they will come to the quilting bee.

Neither the cabinet members nor the prime minister ~~are~~ is going to wave to the crowd.

INDEFINITE PRONOUNS

An **indefinite pronoun** does not refer to a specific person or thing. The following are indefinite pronouns:

all, anybody, anyone, anything, each, either, everybody, everyone, everything, neither, no one, nobody, none, nothing, one, some, somebody, someone, something

Even though many indefinite pronouns seem to refer to more than one person or thing, most require a singular verb. Note especially that *each*, *every*, and words ending in *-body* and *-one* are singular.

Everybody from our class *was* at the nudist colony.

Something in the garage ~~smell~~ smells fishy.

Everyone in our house ~~pay~~ pays credit cards on time.

NEITHER *AND* NONE

When used alone, the indefinite pronouns *neither* and *none* require singular verbs.

Neither *is* correct.

Of the guests who were sent R.S.V.P. invitations, none *has* deigned to respond.

When prepositional phrases with plurals follow the indefinite pronouns *neither* and *none*, in some cases a plural or singular verb may be used. However, it is best to treat *neither* and *none* consistently as singular.

Neither of those flattering adjectives *applies* to my parents.

None of these programs *offers* bonus air miles.

INDEFINITE PRONOUNS THAT CAN BE SINGULAR OR PLURAL

A few indefinite pronouns, such as *all, any, more, most, none,* and *some*, can be singular or plural, depending on the noun or pronoun to which they refer.

> *Singular:* All of the money *is* in a Swiss bank account.
>
> *Plural:* All of his accounts *are* frozen because of the terrorist connection.

COLLECTIVE NOUNS

A collective noun names a class or a group of people or things. Some examples of collective nouns are *band, committee, family, group, jury,* and *team.*

Use a singular verb with the collective noun when you want to communicate that the group is acting as a unit.

> The band *agrees* that it needs a new drummer.
>
> The first-year law class ~~have~~ has a record enrollment.

Use a plural verb when you want to communicate that members of the group are acting independently.

> The original band *have* gone on to pursue solo careers and spend time in rehabilitation centres.
>
> The first-year law class *have* their fingerprints on file.

Sometimes it is better to capture the idea of individual action by recasting the sentence with a plural noun.

> The original band members *have* gone on to pursue solo careers and spend time in rehabilitation centres.

DECIDING WHETHER TO TREAT **NUMBER** *AS A SINGULAR OR PLURAL*

If the collective noun *number* is preceded by *the*, treat it as a singular noun.

> The number of ways to cheat death *is* increasing.

If *number* is preceded by *a*, treat it as a plural.

> A number of Scrabble players *are* getting a triple word score.

UNITS OF MEASUREMENT

Use a singular verb when the unit of measurement is used collectively; that is, when the thing described by the noun cannot be counted.

> One-half of the fat in those French fries *is* unsaturated.

Use a plural verb when the unit of measurement refers to individual persons or things that can be counted.

> Only one-half of your promises *are* likely to be kept.

SUBJECT AFTER VERB

Most often the verb follows the subject in sentences. However, in certain cases, the verb may come before the subject, making it difficult to evaluate subject–verb agreement.

EXPLETIVE CONSTRUCTIONS

Expletive constructions include phrases such as *there is, there are*, or *it is, it was*. When these phrases appear at the beginning of a sentence, the verb often precedes the subject.

> There *are* significant differences among the pop stars of the '60s.

INVERTING SENTENCE ORDER

To achieve sentence variety, you may from time to time wish to invert traditional subject–verb order. Ensure that when you do this, you check that the subject and the verb agree.

> Nestled on the couch ~~is~~ are a beautiful black malamute and a spectacular red setter.

SUBJECT COMPLEMENT

A subject complement is a noun or adjective that follows a linking verb and renames or describes the sentence subject, as in *Elvis Presley is a cult figure*. Because of its relationship to the subject, the complement can often be mistaken for the subject and result in subject–verb agreement errors.

> The socialite's central concern ~~are~~ is facial lines.

> The advice column and the comics ~~is~~ are all I read in the newspaper.

WITH RELATIVE PRONOUNS

WHO, WHICH, *AND* THAT

A relative pronoun such as *who, which,* or *that* usually introduces an adjective clause that modifies the subject. The relative pronoun must agree with its antecedent. The antecedent is the noun or pronoun to which the relative pronoun refers. Thus, the verb must agree with the antecedent.

> The wealthy industrialist who *donates* money to the food bank expects a tax deduction.

CONSTRUCTIONS USING ONE OF THE *AND* ONLY ONE OF THE

Subject–verb agreement mistakes are often made with relative pronouns when the sentence contains *one of the* or *only one of the*.

Generally, with constructions using *one of the*, use a plural verb.

> The stiletto heel is *one of the* kinds of footwear that ~~causes~~ cause a lot of medical problems.

Generally, with *only one of the* constructions, use a singular verb.

> The roller coaster is *only* one *of the* rides that ~~are~~ is featured at Canada's Wonderland.

PLURAL FORM, SINGULAR MEANING

Some words ending in -ics or -s are singular in meaning, even though they are plural in appearance. These words include the following:

athletics, economics, ethics, physics, politics, statistics, mathematics, measles, mumps, news

Nouns such as the above generally require a singular verb.

> Measles ~~were~~ was causing the kindergarten class to miss school.

When nouns such as *mathematics, physics,* and *statistics* refer to a particular item of knowledge, as opposed to the collective body of knowledge, they are treated as plural.

> Environment Canada statistics *reveal* that the area experienced record amounts of smog.

TITLES AND WORDS AS WORDS

A work referred to by its title is treated as a singular entity, even if the title includes a plural word.

> deals
>
> Dog Days ~~deal~~ with the hilarious consequences of Peter's disenchantment with his job.

> describes
>
> *Illegal Aliens* ~~describe~~ people who enter the country without following prescribed immigration procedures.

Adverbs and Adjectives

Adverbs and adjectives are modifiers. Adjectives modify nouns and pronouns. Adverbs can modify

- verbs

  He left the examination *early.*

- adjectives

  Her cheeks were *slightly* red.

- other adverbs

  They left the coffee shop *very* late.

Many adverbs end in -ly (*walk* **quickly**); however, some do not (*walk* **often**). As well, a number of adjectives end in -ly.

That is a *lovely* vase.

Problems can occur when adjectives are incorrectly used as adverbs or vice versa. The best way to decide whether a modifier should be an adjective or an adverb is to determine its function in the sentence. If you are in doubt about whether a word is an adjective or an adverb, you might also consult a good Canadian dictionary.

ADVERBS

In modifying a verb, another adverb, or an adjective, an adverb answers questions such as the following: Why? When? Where? How? The following are some common misuses of adjectives in situations where adverbs are required:

1. incorrectly using adjectives to modify verbs

> loudly clearly
>
> The choir sang ~~loud~~ and ~~clear~~ at the concert.

2. incorrectly using the adjective *good* when the adverb *well* is required

   The minister of education indicated to the media that he wants students within the province to be able to write ~~good~~ well.

   For more detail on the correct uses of *good* and *well*, see page 152 of the usage glossary at the back of this guide.

3. incorrectly using adjectives to modify adjectives or adverbs

   The museum in Niagara Falls has a ~~real~~ really unusual collection of artifacts.

ADJECTIVES

Usually adjectives come before the nouns they modify.

She watched the red dawn.

However, adjectives can also function as subject complements that follow a linking verb. The subject complement renames or describes the sentence subject.

Silence is golden.

Linking verbs communicate states of being as opposed to actions.

The milk at the back of the refrigerator tasted ~~sourly~~ sour.

She feels ~~happily~~ happy.

With storm clouds mounting, the weather looked ~~badly~~ bad.

Some verbs, such as *look, feel, smell,* and *taste,* may or may not be linking verbs. When the word after the verb modifies the subject, the verb is a linking verb, and this modifying word should be an adjective. However, when the word modifies the verb, it should be an adverb.

When the Modifier Is an Adjective
The girl looked curious.

When the Modifier Is an Adverb
The girl looked curiously at the man dressed in a bunny suit.

COMPARATIVES AND SUPERLATIVES

Most adjectives and adverbs have three forms:

1. the positive
2. the comparative
3. the superlative

FORMING COMPARATIVES AND SUPERLATIVES

Adjectives

POSITIVE	COMPARATIVE	SUPERLATIVE
With one- and most two-syllable adjectives		
red	redder	reddest
crazy	crazier	craziest
With longer adjectives		
intoxicating	more intoxicating	most intoxicating
selfish	less selfish	least selfish
A few adjectives are irregular.		
good	better	best
bad	worse	worst
Some have no comparative or superlative form.		
unique	–	–
pregnant	–	–

Adverbs

POSITIVE	COMPARATIVE	SUPERLATIVE
With adverbs ending in *-ly*		
selfishly	more selfishly	most selfishly
gracefully	less gracefully	least gracefully
With other adverbs		
fast	faster	fastest
hard	harder	hardest
A few adverbs are irregular.		
well	better	best
badly	worse	worst
Some have no comparative or superlative form.		
really	–	–
solely	–	–

WHEN TO USE THE COMPARATIVE FORM AND WHEN TO USE THE SUPERLATIVE FORM

When comparing two entities, use the comparative form.

> Which is the ~~least~~ lesser of the two evils?

> The jaguar moves ~~quickest~~ quicker than the lion.

When comparing three or more entities, use the superlative.

> Of the three playwrights, I feel that William Shakespeare is the *greatest*.

> She is among the ~~selfishest~~ most selfish people I know.

DO NOT USE DOUBLE COMPARATIVES OR SUPERLATIVES

> Of the two playwrights, I feel that William Shakespeare is the ~~more~~ greater.

> The painting is probably one of the most ~~beautifulest~~ beautiful in the museum.

DO NOT USE COMPARATIVES OR SUPERLATIVES WITH ABSOLUTE CONCEPTS

Absolute concepts by their very nature do not come in degrees and cannot be compared. Some examples of absolute concepts are *favourite, unique, perfect, pregnant, impossible, infinite,* or *priceless*. If three diamonds are perfect, one cannot be more perfect than the other two.

> *Incorrect:* The cat looked <u>more pregnant</u> than she did last week.

> *Correct:* The cat's pregnancy was more obvious this week.

> That painting by da Vinci is ~~very~~ unique.

> The bizarre comedy was the most ~~unique~~ unusual I have ever seen.

DOUBLE NEGATIVES

Two negatives are acceptable in a sentence only if they create a positive meaning.

> She was <u>not disappointed</u> with her ten-game hitting streak.

A **double negative** is a non-standard English construction in which negative modifiers such as *no, not, neither, none, nothing,* and *never* are paired to cancel each other. Double negatives should be avoided in any formal writing.

The government never does nothing to solve the problems affecting the poor.

Barry did not feel ~~nothing~~ anything during his hernia operation.

In standard English, the modifiers *barely*, *hardly*, and *scarcely* are considered negative modifiers. These words should not be paired with words such as *no*, *not*, or *never*.

They could ~~not~~ barely hear the tiny girl speak.

Problems with Modifiers

A modifier is a word, phrase, or clause that describes or limits another word, phrase, or clause within a sentence. Modifiers must be placed carefully and correctly or they will cloud and in some instances destroy sentence meaning. Generally, modifying words should be kept close to the words they modify.

LIMITING MODIFIERS SUCH AS *ONLY, EVEN*

Place limiting words such as *just, even, only, almost, hardly, nearly*, and *merely* directly before the verb they modify.

She nearly *missed* the swim team's practice.

If one of these words modifies another word in the sentence, place the modifier in front of that word.

Incorrect: In the first quarter, Vince Carter did not even score one point.

Correct: In the first quarter, Vince Carter did not score even one point.

Incorrect: Louis Cyr only weighed 113 kg.

Correct: Louis Cyr weighed only 113 kg.

The modifier *not* is often misplaced, a situation that can create confusing or unintended meanings.

Incorrect/Unintended Meaning: All snakebites are not lethal.

Correct/Intended Meaning: Not all snakebites are lethal.

MISPLACED PHRASES AND CLAUSES

A **misplaced modifier** is a describing word, phrase, or clause that is incorrectly positioned within a sentence, making the modifier's meaning illogical or unclear. The misplaced modifier relates to, or modifies, the wrong word or words in the sentence. When a modifier is misplaced, unusual misreadings can result.

Incorrect: Jennifer sat waiting for her boyfriend to park the car in a slinky red dress with a plunging neckline.

Correct: Jennifer sat waiting in a slinky red dress with a plunging neckline for her boyfriend to park the car.

Incorrect: The counter clerk at the soda fountain brought the sundae to the eager young boy covered in chocolate sauce.

Correct: The counter clerk at the soda fountain brought the sundae covered in chocolate sauce to the eager young boy.

Incorrect: A beautiful painting attracts the viewer's eye on the wall of the National Gallery.

Correct: A beautiful painting on the wall of the National Gallery attracts the viewer's eye.

Sometimes modifier placement can cause the reader to misinterpret the writer's intention. The correction chosen will depend on the writer's intended meaning.

Ambiguous: The fellow we interviewed at the station often talked to us about the weather.

Clear: The fellow we often interviewed at the station talked to us about the weather.

Clear: The fellow we interviewed at the station talked to us often about the weather.

AWKWARDLY PLACED MODIFIERS

Sentences should generally flow in a pattern from subject to verb to object. Keep the subject as close as possible to the main verb and, where possible, don't separate the subject from the main verb of the sentence with a modifying adverb clause.

Awkward: The dog, after chasing the mail carrier, wagged its tail and pranced triumphantly to the front porch.

Clear: The dog wagged its tail and pranced triumphantly to the front porch <u>after chasing the mail carrier</u>.

As well, keep auxiliary verbs near to the main verbs.

Awkward: We have <u>never before</u> had such an apathetic response to our poster campaign.

Clear: We <u>never before</u> have had such an apathetic response to our poster campaign.

SPLIT INFINITIVES

An infinitive consists of *to* and the verb, as in *to love*, *to leave*, and *to forget*. In a **split infinitive**, a modifier is placed between *to* and the verb. Frequently, a split infinitive will make a sentence awkward, and the sentence will need to be revised.

Awkward: Financial analysts expected the stock prices *to*, after a period of sharp decline, dramatically *rise*.

Clear: Financial analysts expected the stock prices *to rise* dramatically after a period of sharp decline.

Awkward: Try *to*, if you can get it, *see* her latest DVD.

Clear: Try *to see* her latest DVD, if you can get it.

However, in a few instances, split infinitives are preferable to alternative wordings.

In *My Big Fat Greek Wedding*, the director attempts <u>*to*</u> convincingly <u>*make*</u> the Toronto setting look like Chicago.

Generally, avoid split infinitives in formal writing.

DANGLING MODIFIERS

A **dangling modifier** is a word, phrase, or clause that does not relate to any word within the sentence and, as a result, confuses the reader. Dangling modifiers usually appear at the start of the sentence and can be one of the following:

- a participial phrase

  <u>Strolling on the beach,</u> a surfer wearing a Speedo suit was seen.

- a gerund phrase

  <u>After eating dinner,</u> the turkey and dressing were left sitting on the table.

- an infinitive phrase

  <u>To win first place on a reality-TV show</u>, stamina is required.

- an elliptical clause

  Keep stirring the stew until thick.

To repair dangling modifier problems, use one of the following revision strategies:

1. PROVIDE THE SUBJECT OF THE SENTENCE IMMEDIATELY AFTER THE DANGLING PHRASE

Dangling Participial Phrase: Strolling on the beach, a surfer wearing a Speedo suit was seen.

Correction: Strolling on the beach, he noticed a surfer wearing a Speedo suit.

2. PROVIDE A SUBJECT FOR THE DANGLING PHRASE

Dangling Gerund Phrase: After eating dinner, the turkey and dressing were left sitting on the table.

Correction: After eating dinner, we left the turkey and dressing sitting on the table.

3. REVISE THE SENTENCE BY CHANGING THE SUBJECT

Dangling Infinitive Phrase: To win first place on a reality-TV show, stamina is required.

Correction: To win first place on a reality-TV show, one requires stamina.

Elliptical Clause: Keep stirring the stew until thick.

Correction: Keep stirring the stew until it is thick.

To assess whether or not a sentence you have written has a dangling modifier, apply the following questioning strategy:

- Does the participial phrase suggest an action without indicating who is performing the action?
  - ❑ NO. You do not have a dangling modifier problem.
  - ❑ YES. *Answer the following question.*
- Does the subject of the independent clause indicate who performs the action?
  - ❑ YES. You do not have a dangling modifier problem.
  - ❑ NO. *Apply one of the three strategies listed above to address the dangling modifier problem.*

Shifts

A **shift** is a sudden and unnecessary change in point of view, verb tense, mood, or voice, or a change from indirect to direct questions or quotations. Shifts can occur within and between sentences. They often blur meaning and confuse readers.

POINT OF VIEW

In writing, **point of view** is the perspective from which the work is written. Often this is indicated by the pronouns the writer uses.

1. First person: I, *we*
2. Second person: *you*
3. Third person: *he/she/it/one* or *they*

You have probably noticed the following in the course of your own writing and reading:

- The first-person point of view often appears in more informal types of writing, such as journals, diaries, and personal letters.
- The second-person point of view is often found in directions or instructional types of writing, such as this handbook.
- The third-person point of view emphasizes the subject. It is used in informative writing, including the writing you do in many academic and professional contexts.

Shifts in point of view occur when a writer begins his or her piece of writing in one point of view and then shifts carelessly back and forth to other points of view. To prevent needless shifts, think about the most appropriate point of view for your writing situation, establish that point of view in your writing, and keep to the point of view.

Shifts in Point of View

Some people, when outfitting their dogs, will have them carry their food. Thus, as ~~our~~ their journey progresses, and stops are periodically made for meals or snacks, the dog's pack becomes lighter.

Your fax machine supports both tone (or multifrequency) and pulse (or rotary) dialling. It is initially set to TONE, so ~~one does~~ you do not need to change the setting if ~~he or she uses~~ you use that kind of line. If you are using a pulse dial line, ~~one~~ you can change the setting to PULSE by following these steps.

A common problem among student writers is shifting from the third-person singular to the third-person plural or vice versa.

Shift from Singular to Plural

Since malamutes have very heavy fur coats, ~~it prefers~~ they prefer to sleep outside even in extremely cold weather.

VERB TENSE

The verb tense tells the reader when the action in the piece of writing is taking place. Shifting from one verb tense to another, without a sound reason, only confuses the reader.

Tense Shift

He is so vain that he always sits at a restaurant table facing the sunlight, since he ~~thought~~ thinks the rays might add to his precious tan.

Student writers often shift tenses when writing about literature. The convention in essays about literature is to describe fictional events consistently in the present tense.

Shift from Literary Present

As an egocentric, Gabriel has "restless eyes" early in "The Dead." However, when he displays empathy near the end of the story, he ~~possessed~~ possesses "curious eyes."

VERB MOOD AND VOICE

MOOD

Shifts can also occur in the mood of verbs. The mood of the verb indicates the manner of action. There are three moods in English:

1. The indicative mood is used to state facts or opinions, or to ask questions.

   He wrote a short story.

   Did he win a prize for the story?

2. The imperative mood is used to give a command or advice, or make a request.

   Don't do that!

   Rewind the videotape before returning it.

3. The subjunctive mood is used to express doubt, wishes, or possibility.

   If I were lucky, I might have won the lottery.

Mood Shift

Include more foreground than background by focusing closer than your main subject while keeping the subject within the depth of field. ^ ~~The reverse is also true.~~

Include more background by focusing farther than your main subject.

VOICE

Voice refers to whether a verb is active or passive. A verb is active when the subject is the doer of the action. A verb is passive when the subject of the verb receives the action. If the writer suddenly shifts between voices, it can be jarring and confusing to the reader.

Shift in Voice

I could immediately comprehend the devastation of the avalanche as soon as ^ the turn opening to the valley ~~was made~~.

I made

INDIRECT TO DIRECT QUESTIONS OR QUOTATIONS

DIRECT AND INDIRECT QUOTATIONS

In a direct quotation, the writer repeats a speaker's words exactly, placing those words within quotation marks. In an indirect quotation, the writer summarizes or paraphrases what the speaker has said.

Direct Quotation: U.S. General William C. Westmoreland said, "We'll blow them back into the Stone Age."

Indirect Quotation: U.S. General William C. Westmoreland said his forces would bomb the enemy so relentlessly that they would be blown back into the Stone Age.

Shift from Indirect to Direct

told me to

The dog trainer ~~indicated that I should~~ keep Pepé by my side

not

and ~~don't~~ give the dog more than a foot of slack on his lead.

DIRECT AND INDIRECT QUESTIONS

A direct question is one that is asked directly.

Which road do you take to get to Lions Head?

An indirect question reports that a question was asked, but does not ask it.

I asked which road to take to get to Lions Head.

Shifting from indirect to direct questions can make writing awkward and confusing.

Shift from Indirect to Direct

I asked if they wanted to hike the Bruce Trail, and if so, whether they would like ~~do they want~~ to start at Tobermory or St. Catharines.

Mixed Constructions

A sentence with a **mixed construction** incorrectly changes from one grammatical construction to another, incompatible, one, thereby confusing the sentence's meaning.

MIXED GRAMMAR

When you draft a sentence, your options for structuring that sentence are limited by the grammatical patterns of English. You must consistently follow the pattern you choose within the sentence. You cannot start the sentence using one grammatical pattern and then abruptly change to another. *Don't switch horses* [grammatical structures] *in the middle of a stream* [sentence] is an idiom that can help you remember this key grammatical guideline.

Mixed: By multiplying the number of specialty stations available to viewers via digital television increases the chance that cultural communities within Canada's diverse cultural mosaic will be better served.

Revised: Multiplying the number of specialty stations available to viewers via digital television increases the chance that cultural communities within Canada's diverse cultural mosaic will be better served.

OR

Revised: By multiplying the number of specialty stations available to viewers via digital television, satellite and cable companies increase the chance that cultural communities within Canada's diverse cultural mosaic will be better served.

Another mixed construction problem is incorrectly combining clauses.

Satellite ~~Although satellite~~ dishes have become popular in many northern Canadian communities, but many viewers still prefer local stations.

From time to time, when revising your own work, you may encounter a sentence that can't be fixed grammatically. In instances such as this, it is often wise to rethink what you want to say and then recast the sentence so it is clear, straightforward, and logical.

Mixed: In communicative language teaching, students' errors are corrected only when they interfere with comprehension rather than by the direct method in which students' errors are corrected immediately to avoid habit formation.

Revised: In communicative language teaching, students' errors are corrected only when they interfere with comprehension; <u>in the direct method, students' errors are corrected immediately</u> to avoid habit formation.

ILLOGICAL CONNECTIONS

A number of sentence faults can occur when elements of the sentence do not logically fit together. **Faulty predication** is one example of such a problem. In faulty predication, the subject and predicate do not make sense together. To remedy this problem, either the subject or the predicate must be revised.

Originally,
~~The original function of~~ the Internet was created to exchange academic and military information.

The decisions on who would make Canada's 2002 Olympic
were made
hockey team ~~was chosen~~ by a management committee headed by Wayne Gretzky.

An appositive is a noun or noun phrase that renames or explains a noun or noun phrase immediately before it.

November, <u>the month of my birth</u>, . . .

The appositive must logically relate to the noun or noun phrase that precedes it; otherwise, **faulty apposition** occurs.

speculation
Stock ~~speculators~~, a <u>very risky business</u>, demands nerves of steel and a healthy bank account.

AVOIDING *IS WHEN, IS WHERE, REASON . . . IS BECAUSE*

In formal writing, avoid the following constructions:

1. *is when* or *is where*

In computer dating,
~~Computer dating is when~~ a computer is used to match potential romantic partners according to their compatibility, interests, and desirability.

2. *the reason . . . is because*

~~The reason~~ I watch horror movies ~~is~~ because I need a release from the tensions of life.

These constructions are not grammatical and often add unnecessary words to a sentence. If you find such constructions in your drafts, revise the sentences that contain them.

Parallelism

Parallelism in writing means that equal grammatical structures are used to express equal ideas. Errors in parallelism, known as **faulty parallelism**, occur when unequal structures are used to express equal ideas. Words, phrases, and clauses should all be parallel when they express a similar idea and perform a similar function in a sentence. When using parallelism for effect, balance single words with single words, phrases with phrases, and clauses with clauses.

Parallel, Balanced Elements

Words: There are three sides to every story—yours, mine, and all that lie between.

—*Jody Kern*

Phrases: Do what you can, with what you have, where you are.

—*Theodore Roosevelt*

Clauses: Think like a man of action, act like a man of thought.

—*Henri Bergson*

WITH ITEMS IN A SERIES

When the reader encounters items in a series, he or she expects a parallel grammatical pattern to be maintained within the sentence. However, when one or more items do not follow the parallel grammatical pattern, the sentence seems jarring and awkward to the reader.

Awkward: Anatole liked the lawn, the hedge, and to garden.

Correction: Anatole liked <u>the lawn, the hedge, and the garden</u>.

Awkward: Ace may not be the cutest or the largest dog in existence, but he's also very smart.

Correction: Ace may not be the <u>cutest</u> or the <u>largest</u> dog in existence, but he may be one of the <u>smartest</u>.

Awkward: Being outdoors, feeling the winds off the ocean, and to smell the Douglas fir are what I like about hiking British Columbia's West Coast Trail.

Correction: Being outdoors, feeling the winds off the ocean, and smelling the Douglas fir are what I like about hiking British Columbia's West Coast Trail.

WITH PAIRED ITEMS

Parallel ideas are often connected in one of three ways:

1. with a coordinating conjunction, such as *or, and,* or *but*
2. with a pair of correlative conjunctions, such as *not only . . . but also* or *either . . . or*
3. with comparative constructions using *than* or *as*

Whenever you relate ideas using one of these methods, always emphasize the connection between or among ideas by expressing them in parallel grammatical form.

USING PARALLELISM WITH COORDINATING CONJUNCTIONS

Coordinating conjunctions are words such as *and, but, or, nor, for, yet,* and *so* that connect ideas of equal importance. Avoid faulty parallelism by ensuring that all elements joined by coordinating conjunctions are parallel in grammatical form.

Not Parallel: Alfred, you may go by train, boat, car, bus, or a jet will take you there.

Parallel: Alfred, you may go by train, boat, car, bus, or jet.

Not Parallel: Our debating team read Jordan's ideas, were discussing her arguments, and have decided they are not relevant to our debate position.

Parallel: Our debating team read Jordan's ideas, discussed her arguments, and decided they are not relevant to our debate position.

USING PARALLEL FORMS WITH CORRELATIVE CONJUNCTIONS

Correlative conjunctions are pairs of words that join equal grammatical structures. Examples include *not only . . . but also, either . . . or,* and *both . . . and.* Avoid faulty parallelism by ensuring that each element linked by correlative conjunctions is parallel in its grammatical form.

Not Parallel: The staff of the computer lab not only supported the president's request for a bigger office, but also they were prepared to order a desk, a chair, and a bar for her convenience.

Parallel: The staff of the computer lab supported the president's request not only for a bigger office, but also for a desk, a chair, and a bar for her convenience.

Not Parallel: Either viewers criticized the television station for its inflammatory views, or it was criticized for its political stance.

Parallel: Viewers *criticized* the television station either for its inflammatory views or for its political stance.

COMPARISONS LINKED WITH **THAN** *OR* **AS**

Often you will use *than* or *as* to make comparisons. To avoid faulty parallelism, make sure the elements being compared are expressed using parallel grammatical structure.

Not Parallel: Having great wealth is not as satisfying as the completion of charitable works.

Parallel: Having great wealth is not as satisfying as completing charitable works.

Not Parallel: It is better to give than do the receiving.

Parallel: It is better to give than to receive.

Note: The corrections shown above are just a few of many equally acceptable alternatives. In some instances, faulty parallelism corrections that occur to you may be improvements on the suggestions made here.

STYLE

STYLE

Some aspects of writing are matters of style, not of structure or of meaning. Here, there often are no hard and fast rules, but there are guidelines to help you streamline and clarify your writing to satisfy readers' needs and expectations. In this section you will find helpful advice to make your writing smooth and persuasive.

Wordiness

Effective writing is concise, clear, and direct. Concise writing does not necessarily mean fewer words or shorter sentences. It means words that function clearly and sentences that express their point without empty words. A longer sentence is justified if it is required to express a sophisticated idea. On the other hand, many shorter sentences can be even more economically written. When revising, review each sentence you write with an eye to eliminating any phrase or word that is not absolutely necessary to your intended meaning.

REDUNDANCIES

Redundancy is the use of unnecessary words in a sentence. Often the same idea is expressed twice or more.

> It is 6:30 a.m. in the morning.

Other common redundancies include *final completion, important essentials, close proximity, consensus of opinion,* and *actual fact.*

> ~~The reason~~ Nebuchadnezzar stopped his conquest ~~was~~ because he heard of his father's death and his own succession to the throne.

> The board members did not want to repeat the debate ~~again~~, so they had a frank ~~and honest~~ discussion during which they identified some basic ~~essential~~ ideas.

> When people are in ~~situations of~~ conflict at a meeting, they should ~~try to~~ attempt to ~~form a~~ achieve consensus ~~of opinion~~.

> The bridge ~~that people cross to get~~ to Burlington is ~~sort of~~ rectangular ~~in shape~~, and it is made of strong materials such as reinforced steel~~,~~ and concrete~~, and etc~~.

UNNECESSARY REPETITION OF WORDS

Sometimes you may wish to repeat words or phrases to create an effect or for emphasis, as in parallel constructions. However, when words are repeated for no apparent reason, they make writing seem sloppy and awkward. As you revise, eliminate unnecessary repeated words.

> The quarterback passed the football, but the lineman raised his meaty~~, heavy~~ hand and batted the ~~football~~ ball away.
>
> The houses ~~where the people live~~ are not far from ~~the city of~~ Moncton.

EMPTY OR INFLATED PHRASES

Sometimes, to make your writing sound more important, you may be tempted to include certain phrases you've heard others use. When you examine your sentences carefully, you'll find these phrases only increase your word count and contain little or no meaning. Effective writers state what they mean as simply and directly as possible. As you revise your work, trim sentences of any wordy, empty, or inflated phrases.

> ~~By virtue of the fact that~~ Because ~~at the current time~~ currently we do not have sufficient funding, the skateboard park will not be built.

You can use concise words or phrases without affecting your meaning.

ELIMINATING WORDY OR INFLATED PHRASES

WORDY/INFLATED	CONCISE
along the lines of	like
as a matter of fact	in fact
at all times	always
at the present time	now, currently, presently
at this point in time	now, currently, presently
because of the fact	because
being that	because
by means of	by

WORDY/INFLATED	CONCISE
by virtue of the fact that	because
due to the fact that	because
for the purpose of	for
for the simple reason that	because
have a tendency to	tend
have the ability to	be able to
in the nature of	like
in order to	to
in spite of the fact that	although, even though
in the event that	if
in the final analysis	finally
in the neighbourhood of	about, approximately
in the world of today	today
it is necessary that	must
on the occasion of	when
prior to	before
until such a time as	until
with regard to	about

SIMPLIFYING STRUCTURE

The following word-trimming strategies will help you make your sentences simple, clear, and direct.

STRENGTHEN THE VERB

Often nouns derived from verbs can be turned back into verbs to make the sentence more direct and active.

> accumulated
>
> During the strike, ~~the accumulation of~~ garbage ~~carried on~~ for fifteen days.

AVOID COLOURLESS VERBS

The verbs is, *are*, *was*, *were*, and *have* are weak and often create wordy sentence constructions.

The budget proposal before the legislature ~~is to do with~~ recommends tax cuts and massive reductions in public sector spending.

REVISE EXPLETIVE CONSTRUCTIONS

An expletive construction uses *there* or *it* and a form of the verb *be* in front of the sentence subject. Often these constructions create excess words. You might remove the expletive and revise the sentence to make it more concise and direct.

> ~~There is a~~ A picture of Pierre Trudeau playing baseball ~~that~~ shows the energy he brought to the prime minister's office.

> ~~It is important that~~ Most importantly, you should remain calm if your kayak capsizes in rough water.

WHERE POSSIBLE, USE THE ACTIVE VOICE

The active voice is generally more concise and direct than the passive voice. Use the active voice when you want to be direct and to focus on the action of a sentence.

> *Passive:* The research was conducted by senior students who were planning to enter graduate school.

> *Active:* Senior students who plan to enter graduate school conducted the research.

REDUCING CLAUSES AND PHRASES

In many instances, modifying clauses and phrases can be tightened. Where possible, reduce clauses to phrases and phrases to single words.

> As basketball fans, we journeyed to Almonte, Ontario, ~~which is~~ the birthplace of Canadian John Naismith.

> ~~Loaded with power, the~~ The powerful car was considered unbeatable.

Diction and Audience

The effectiveness of your writing will in large measure depend on the appropriateness of the language you decide to use for your audience. Choose the wording that best suits the context and the audience of your writing. Consider these elements as you choose your words:

- subject
- audience (their needs, expectations, and feelings)
- purpose
- voice (as reflected in your unique writing style)

The following section provides guidance and information that will help you to select appropriate language for your writing assignments.

JARGON

Jargon is the specialized language of a particular group or occupation. In some instances you may need to use jargon, such as when your audience is the particular group or occupation that uses the jargon, or when you can reasonably assume that your audience will understand this specialized language. Generally, though, avoid jargon and use plain English in its place.

Jargon: Positive input into the infrastructure impacts systematically on the functional base of the organization in that it stimulates meaningful objectives from a strategic standpoint.

Revised: Positive feedback to the organization helps it formulate concrete, strategic objectives.

In addition to very specialized language, jargon often includes language that is intended to impress readers rather than to communicate information and ideas effectively. Jargon-filled language is often found in business, government, education, and military documents.

Sentences containing jargon terms are difficult to read and extremely unclear.

Jargon: The Director of Instruction implemented the optimal plan to ameliorate poor test scores among reading-at-risk students.

Clear: The Director of Instruction carried out the best plan to improve poor test scores among students having trouble reading.

Jargon: We will endeavour to facilitate a viable trash recovery initiative for all residences in the neighbourhood.

Clear: We will try to create a workable garbage pickup plan for all neighbourhood homes.

If you encounter inflated words or phrases in your writing draft, consider alternative words that are simple, clear, and precise in meaning.

ELIMINATING JARGON	
WORDS DESIGNED TO IMPRESS	SIMPLE ALTERNATIVES
ameliorate	fix, improve
commence	begin, start
components	parts
endeavour	attempt, try
exit	go, leave
facilitate	help
factor	cause, consideration
finalize	complete, finish
impact on	affect
implement	carry out
indicator	sign
initiate	start, begin
optimal	best
parameters	boundaries, limits
prior to	before
prioritize	order, rank
utilize	use
viable	workable

PRETENTIOUS LANGUAGE, EUPHEMISMS

AVOID PRETENTIOUS LANGUAGE

When writing for academic audiences and purposes, it is tempting to opt for elevated language. However, using uncommon or unnecessarily long words can highlight rather than obscure deficiencies in content—and make the writing seem pretentious. Academic writing does not require that you use longer, difficult words for their own sake. State your ideas in words that you are sure your audience will understand.

Pretentious: It is *de rigueur* to expound on reification in Timothy Findley's fictional tome *The Wars*.

Plain Language: It is necessary to discuss the treatment of people as objects in Timothy Findley's novel *The Wars*.

AVOID EUPHEMISMS

A **euphemism** is a word or expression intended to take the place of harsher or less acceptable words or phrases. An example of a euphemism in a military context is *collateral damage*, a term sometimes used to describe *civilian casualties*. In a few writing situations, using euphemisms is acceptable. For instance, when expressing condolences to a friend you might use the euphemism *passed away* as a substitute for *died*. Generally, however, avoid euphemisms because they are highly indirect and blur meaning.

AVOIDING EUPHEMISMS

EUPHEMISM	PLAIN ENGLISH
chemical dependency	drug addiction
correctional facility	jail
declared redundant	laid off
developing nations	poor countries
downsizing	laying off or firing employees
economically deprived	poor
incendiary device	bomb
laid to rest	buried
leather-like	vinyl
military solution	war
misleading phrase	lie
pre-owned automobile	used car
starter home	small house
strategic withdrawal	defeat or retreat

SLANG, REGIONALISMS, NON-STANDARD ENGLISH

SLANG

Slang is the informal, colourful vocabulary that is often unique to and coined by subgroups such as teenagers, college students, musicians, skateboarders, computer programmers, street gangs, rap artists, and soldiers. Slang is often used to communicate the unique common experiences of these subgroups, and it is frequently not understood by all segments of society. Most often, slang attempts to be current and trendy, but such language is soon over-used and quickly becomes dated. For instance, in the early part of the twentieth century, the expression *the cat's pyjamas* was the fashionable way to call something or someone *excellent*; more recently, a *cool dude* might use the slang terms *bad* and *wicked*. Other more modern examples of slang include *bummer, grunt, rip-off, wired*, or *preppie*.

Slang can often make story dialogue sound lively and authentic. However, it is inappropriate in formal writing such as academic essays and business letters.

> Jeff ~~flunked~~ failed his final history ~~exam~~ examination, and now his semester ~~is a total write off~~ has been completely wasted.

> *Slang:* Mel and her gang are coming over and we're going to watch the tube and pig out.

> *Formal:* Melanie and her friends are coming over. We are going to watch television and eat snacks.

REGIONAL EXPRESSIONS

A regional expression is common to a particular area of the country. For instance, in Atlantic Canada, a *barachois* is "a tidal pond partly obstructed by a bar" (*Nelson Canadian Dictionary*).

> Murray could see the skiff beyond the <u>barachois</u>.

Regional expressions, like slang, can add colour and authenticity; however, they may not be familiar to a general audience and should be avoided in formal academic writing.

> After he caught the winning salmon, they threw the fisherman into the ~~salt chuck~~ ocean.

Salt chuck is a regional expression used in British Columbia and the U.S. Pacific Northwest. It might not be known to all Canadians.

Many Canadian dictionaries specify whether a word or expression is regional.

NON-STANDARD ENGLISH

Non-standard English is acceptable in informal social and regional contexts, but it should be avoided in formal writing.

Examples of non-standard English include the following words and phrases from the Glossary of Usage at the back of this guide:

ain't, anyways, bursted, hisself, nowheres, theirselves

Standard English, on the other hand, is the written English commonly expected and used in educational institutions, businesses, government, and other contexts in which people must formally communicate with one another. Use standard English in all of your academic writing. If you are in doubt about whether a word or phrase is standard or non-standard English, check the Glossary of Usage at the back of this guide or a good Canadian dictionary.

Non-Standard: The guy was nowheres in sight, and he could of left town, but she didn't care anyways.

Standard: The man was nowhere in sight. He could have left town, but she did not care anyway.

LEVELS OF FORMALITY

Informal writing is casual in language and tone, and it is appropriate for communication in such forms as notes, friendly letters, e-mails, journal entries, and brief memorandums to people you know well.

Formal writing is formal in tone and language, and it is appropriate for academic and business writing such as essays, research reports, job application letters, and business letters and reports.

When deciding which level of formality to use in your writing, you should consider two key factors:

1. subject
2. audience

As you draft and revise your work, ask the following questions about the level of formality you select.

SUBJECT

- Is my choice of words appropriate to the seriousness of my subject?

AUDIENCE

- What type of language will my audience expect?
- Is my choice of words appropriate for the intended audience?
- Does my choice of words and the tone these words create make me seem too close or too distant from my readers?

In academic or business writing, use a formal level of writing and assume a serious tone. The following opening line of a career application letter is too informal.

> *Too Informal:* I'm just dropping you a few lines to put my name in for that fisheries biologist's assistant job I saw somewhere in the *Free Press* a few weeks back.

> *More Formal:* I am writing to apply for the fisheries biologist's assistant position advertised in the June 16 edition of the *Free Press.*

The level of language can also seem inappropriate when it is too formal.

> *Too Formal:* When the illustrious Maple Leafs exited from the frozen playing surface trailing their less renowned opponents, the Wild, by the modest score of 1–0, the assembled spectators vigorously voiced their disapproval. The officials in charge of the National Hockey League were authentic demons for having the audacity to schedule these mismatched contests between the annual All-Star Game and the hockey tournament that is part of Olympic competition.

> *More Appropriate:* When the Leafs left the ice trailing the Wild 1–0, loud boos erupted from the crowd. The NHL was the real culprit for scheduling lopsided games like these between the All-Star Game and the Olympics.

NONSEXIST LANGUAGE

Sexist language is biased in attributing characteristics and roles to people exclusively on the basis of gender. Sometimes sexist language is very obvious, but often it is less so. Sexist language can be explicit, as in calling an attractive young woman a *hot chick*. It can be patronizing by referring to a mature woman as a *girl Friday*. It can reflect stereotypical thinking by unnecessarily drawing attention to a person's gender, as in a *female university president*. And sexist language can be subtle, yet still highly biased, by including only male pronouns when more inclusive language is needed; for example, *an athlete always needs to maintain his composure.*

Sexist language can apply to men as well as women, for instance, if a writer describes *a male kindergarten teacher.*

There are a number of strategies you might employ to avoid sexist language.

1. Treat all people equally in your descriptions of them.

   Unequal Treatment: Mr. Delmonico, Mr. Habib, Mr. Dawson, and Tillie, the secretary, arrived for the meeting.

   Acceptable: Mr. Delmonico, Mr. Habib, Mr. Dawson, and Ms. Lord arrived for the meeting.

2. Avoid stereotypes.

   Stereotyping: Like all men, he hates to cook.

3. Use pairs of pronouns to indicate inclusive gender references.

   Exclusive: A professor is motivated by his students.

   Acceptable: A professor is motivated by his or her students.

4. Rewrite the sentence as a plural.

   Acceptable: Professors are motivated by their students.

5. Rewrite the sentence so there is no gender problem.

   Acceptable: A professor is motivated by students.

6. Make gender-neutral word choices.

AVOIDING SEXIST LANGUAGE

INAPPROPRIATE	GENDER-NEUTRAL
alderman	city council member, councillor
anchorman	anchor
businessman	businessperson, entrepreneur
chairman	chairperson, chair
clergyman	member of the clergy, minister
coed	student
craftsman	artisan, craftsperson
fireman	firefighter
forefather	ancestor
foreman	supervisor
freshman	first-year student
housewife	homemaker

INAPPROPRIATE	GENDER-NEUTRAL
mailman	mail carrier, letter carrier, postal worker
male nurse	nurse
mankind	people, humankind, human
manpower	personnel, human resources
newsman	journalist, reporter
policeman	police officer
salesman	salesperson, sales clerk
stewardess	flight attendant
to man	to staff, to operate
weatherman	weather forecaster
waitress	server
workman	worker, labourer, employee

CONNOTATIONS

Many words have two levels of meaning: a **denotative** meaning and a **connotative** meaning. The denotative meaning of a word is its common, literal, dictionary meaning. The connotative meaning is the emotional meaning of the word, which includes experiences and associations you make when you see a word in print or hear it spoken. For example, the dictionary meaning of *eagle* is "a large bird of prey." However, the word *eagle* also carries additional emotional and associative meanings such as "power," "pride," "majesty," and "fierceness."

When considering any word for a piece of writing, you should consider both its denotative and connotative meanings. Sometimes by using a word with certain connotations, you could imply a meaning you do not intend. Conversely, you can enhance your intended meaning by selecting the word with the most appropriate connotations for your subject, purpose, and audience. Often, reviewing all listed meanings in a dictionary entry will give you a sense of a word's connotations.

> The young women ~~giggled~~ laughed at all the right parts in the Restoration comedy.

Giggled has an association with immaturity, and since the women were *young*, the sentence implies the women were immature. The intended meaning of the sentence was that the women appreciated the humour of the play, so *laughed* is more appropriate.

> Ethel ~~is a victim of~~ has rheumatoid arthritis and has ~~suffered from~~ had it for ten years.

It is even better to use this sentence instead: *Ethel was diagnosed with rheumatoid arthritis ten years ago.* Other emotional language related to suffering is best avoided since this kind of language adds an inappropriate slant to the meaning.

NOUNS

There are many types of nouns.

GENERAL AND SPECIFIC NOUNS

Nouns can be very general or very specific. Suppose a friend asks, *What did you do on Saturday?* You respond: *I watched a comedy*. *Comedy* is a very broad, general noun. Your response could refer to a sophisticated Shakespearean comedy, a television situation comedy, or a particular movie, such as *Ace Ventura: Pet Detective*. All of these individual alternatives within the general category *comedy* are specific nouns.

ABSTRACT AND CONCRETE NOUNS

Nouns can be abstract or concrete. Abstract nouns refer to concepts, ideas, qualities, and conditions. They are not concrete, for instance, *love, charity, kindness, humanism, youth,* and *integrity*. Concrete nouns name things that are detectable by your senses, for instance, *snake, dill, sunset, coffee, caramel,* and *harp*.

Many professional writers, especially poets and novelists, spend a great deal of time selecting the most appropriate and precise word to communicate an idea or feeling. Similarly, in your own writing, try to select the most effective word for your purpose. Of course, in the range of your writing assignments you will frequently need to describe, explain, and evaluate general and abstract content. At these times, general and abstract language will be most appropriate. But wherever possible, use specific and concrete nouns to make your writing clear and evocative.

> ~~Hazy city air~~ Toronto's smog made it difficult to breathe as we ~~put the boat in the water~~ launched the sailboat onto Lake Ontario.

General abstract nouns, such as *things*, *considerations*, and *aspects*, are extremely vague and lacking in colour.

have several renovations done

We plan to ~~do a number of things~~ to improve our home.

issues to discuss

There are several ~~considerations to be addressed~~ before we allow the new subdivision.

ACTIVE VERBS

Where possible, choose precise verbs that give your writing impact and power.

WHICH VERBS ARE WEAK?

Weak verbs are forms of the verb to be (*be, am, is, are, was, were, being, been*). None of these verb forms communicates a specific action. As well, verbs in the passive voice tend to be lacking in power. Combine the two—the *be* verb and the passive voice—and you have lifeless, uninspiring writing: *An acceptable job was done by her.*

HOW CAN I USE VERBS TO MAKE MY WRITING LIVELY?

Choose precise, vigorous, emphatic, expressive, or descriptive verbs in the active voice. In the following examples, the student has revised his or her sentence from one using the verb *be* in the passive voice to a precise verb in the active voice.

Using **Be** *Verb:* The dynamic acting coach *was charged* with the training of the eager young actors.

Passive Voice: The eager young actors *were trained* by the dynamic acting coach.

Active Voice: The dynamic acting coach *trained* the eager young actors.

Use the most precise and descriptive verbs to vividly communicate the action(s) performed in your sentence.

approached

As she ~~got near to~~ the finish line, the marathon runner

lunged for grimaced collapsed

~~leaned toward~~ the tape, ~~crinkled her face~~, and ~~fell down~~.

WHEN SHOULD I REPLACE THE **BE** *VERB?*

Change the *be* verb form when it creates a wordy construction. Look for a word that could be turned into a verb in the phrase following the *be* verb.

infringe on

Keeping the prisoners in cages would ~~be an infringement of~~ their human rights.

WHEN SHOULD I NOT REPLACE THE **BE** *VERB?*

1. You should keep forms of *be* (*be, am, is, are, was, were, being, been*) when you want to link the subject of a sentence with a noun that renames the subject or an adjective that describes it.

   Life *is* a bed of roses.

   Bed-and-breakfast proprietors *are* usually hospitable.

2. Keep *be* verb forms when they function as helping verbs before present participles.

   The elk *are* vanishing.

3. The *be* verb forms are acceptable when expressing ongoing action.

   I *was driving* to work when I heard that the serial murderer *had been convicted.*

WHEN SHOULD I REPLACE A PASSIVE VERB?

With sentences in the active voice, the subject performs the action.

Active Voice: José *hammered* the nail.

With sentences in the passive voice, the subject receives the action.

Passive Voice: The nail *was hammered* by José.

In some passive sentences the performer of the action is not mentioned.

The nail was hammered.

Strong writing clearly states who or what performs actions. Use the active voice by making the person or thing that performs the action the subject of the sentence.

The class selected

^"Canada's Ethnic Diversity" ~~was selected by the class~~ as the theme for the panel discussion.

WHEN SHOULD I NOT REPLACE A PASSIVE VERB?

Use the passive voice in the following writing situations:

1. You want to emphasize who or what receives the action.
2. You want to give less emphasis to the person or thing that performs the action.
3. The person or thing that performs the action is not known.

For example, in the communication situation involving José and the nail, you would select the active voice if you wished to emphasize José's importance. If you wanted to emphasize the importance of the nail being hammered, you would use the passive voice. And if hammering the nail was of central importance and José of no importance whatsoever, or if you didn't know who did the hammering, you would use *The nail was hammered.*

MISUSED WORDS

Often when working on a draft, you may want to use a word but may be unsure of the word's meaning or spelling. Always check the meaning of such words in a good dictionary. Misusing words can obscure your overall meaning and create unintentional humour.

> Burns is ~~conscience~~ conscious of his own powers of destruction.

> The provincial review committee ~~censured~~ censored the pornographic movie.

> In a definitive book on Gorbachev, the author ~~sighted~~ cited the main reasons for the collapse of the Soviet Union.

Many writers incorrectly use a noun when the meaning and sentence structure require an adjective. For instance, *abhorrence, indulgence,* or *independence* are used, respectively, when sentences require the adjective forms *abhorrent, indulgent,* or *independent.*

> It is an ~~abhorrence~~ abhorrent practice when advertisers target viewers under five years of age.

STANDARD IDIOMS

An **idiom** is an expression whose meaning cannot be determined simply by knowing the definition of each word within the idiom. Many idioms are very colourful and easy to spot: *kill two birds with one stone, read between the lines, the last straw.*

An idiom always appears in one particular form, one that may not necessarily be taken literally. An example of an idiom is *beside himself* [or *herself*]. *She was beside herself* means "She was in a state of extreme excitement or agitation."

Using idiomatic expressions with prepositions can be tricky. An unidiomatic expression may make better literal sense, but the idiomatic expression is used because it is accepted English usage. If you are in doubt, check a good Canadian dictionary by looking up the word before the preposition.

AVOIDING UNIDIOMATIC EXPRESSIONS

UNIDIOMATIC	IDIOMATIC
according with	according to
angry at	angry with
capable to	capable of
comply to	comply with
desirous to	desirous of
different than	different from
go by	go to
intend on doing	intend to do
off of	off
plan on doing	plan to do
preferable than	preferable to
prior than	prior to
recommend her to do	recommend that she do
superior than	superior to
sure and	sure to
try and	try to
type of a	type of
wait on a person	wait for a person
wait on line	wait in line
with reference in	with reference to

CLICHÉS

A **cliché** is an overused phrase or expression that has become tired and predictable and, hence, is ineffective for freshly communicating writing ideas. Here are some clichés to avoid in your writing:

add insult to injury, at long last, a word to the wise,
cool as a cucumber, cold as ice, easier said than done,
few and far between, first and foremost,
for all intents and purposes, finishing touches,
good as gold, hit the nail on the head, in the long run,
it stands to reason, narrow escape, red-letter day,
this day and age

You might make a database in a computer file of other clichés to avoid.

Clichés, by being so predictable, deprive writing of any sense of surprise. However, in some rare instances, you might inject freshness into a cliché by giving it an unexpected twist.

> He is as strong as an ox; unfortunately, ox-like describes his odour, too.

FIGURES OF SPEECH

In figurative language, words carry more than their literal meaning. **Figures of speech** are particular types of figurative language. Common examples of figures of speech are **similes, personification,** and **metaphors**. In a simile, a comparison is made between two different ideas or objects, using *like* or *as*. In personification, human traits are assigned to something that is not human. And in a metaphor, a comparison is made between two otherwise dissimilar ideas or objects; here, the comparison does not use *like* or *as*.

Used effectively, figures of speech can add colour and emphasis to your writing and enrich meaning. However, used without care, they can make writing clumsy. A common writing problem is mixing metaphors. In a **mixed metaphor**, two or more incongruous images are mingled.

> Harry depth of depression
> ~~The Grand Canyon of Harry's depression~~ reached the ~~pinnacle~~ when his pet died.

PUNCTUATION

PUNCTUATION

Punctuation is an essential part of clear, grammatical writing. It makes your sentences logical and readable, and provides a signal to the reader of how something is to be understood. Punctuation is not just window-dressing—without it, most readers and writers would be hopelessly lost. Although the rules for correct punctuation are quite detailed, they are basically straightforward. This section will help you to master proper punctuation; practice will make it second nature.

The Comma

Frequently, a comma is essential to ensure that readers clearly understand your intended meaning. Omitting or misplacing a comma can easily lead to misreadings.

> While e-mailing,^ Mary Beth spoke on the telephone with her stockbroker.

INDEPENDENT CLAUSES WITH COORDINATING CONJUNCTION

In some sentences, two or more independent clauses (clauses that can stand on their own as sentences) are linked by coordinating conjunctions (*and, or, for, but, so, nor,* and *yet*). In such sentences, place a comma before the coordinating conjunction.

> I enjoy watching television, but I draw the line at World Wrestling Entertainment.

Exception: If the two independent clauses are very short, and there is no chance of misinterpreting the sentence, the comma may be omitted.

> The Greyhound bus pulled in and we boarded it.

INTRODUCTORY ELEMENTS

COMMAS WITH INTRODUCTORY CLAUSES

An introductory adverbial clause is a construction with a subject and a verb that introduces a main clause.

> Whenever he hears gossip about company plans for hiring,^ Pedro talks about his conspiracy theory.

> By a bend in the mighty Thompson River,^ I learned to swim.

If the phrase or clause is very brief, and there is no danger of misreading the sentence, the comma may be omitted.

> In a flash it was over.

COMMAS WITH LONGER INTRODUCTORY PHRASES

After longer introductory phrases, use a comma to indicate that the main part of the sentence is about to start.

After appetizers and a six-course family dinner, my uncle fell asleep in his chair. (prepositional phrase)

Verbal phrases include participles, gerunds, and infinitives.

Elated about the court ruling, Renée phoned her probation officer. (verbal phrase)

By studying the stock market, Rafe found a way to add excitement to his life. (verbal phrase)

To get noticed by a casting director, an actor must first establish a name for herself in local theatre. (infinitive phrase)

Follow an introductory absolute phrase with a comma.

All things considered, it was an ideal first date.

ITEMS IN A SERIES

A series in a sentence could be three or more words, phrases, or clauses that have the same grammatical form and are of equal importance. Place a comma after each item in the series. An item might be one word, a phrase, or a clause.

To function as a freelance writer, he needed a computer, a printer, Internet access, and a partner who would pay the bills.

COORDINATE ADJECTIVES

Coordinate adjectives are two or more adjectives that separately and equally modify the noun or pronoun. The order of these adjectives can be changed without affecting the meaning of the sentence. Coordinate adjectives can be joined by *and*. Separate coordinate adjectives with commas.

The cold, smelly, wet basement was off-limits to the children as a play area.

It was a fluffy, playful, tiny kitten.

CUMULATIVE ADJECTIVES

Cumulative adjectives modify the adjective after them and a noun or pronoun. Cumulative adjectives increase meaning from word to word as they progress toward the noun or pronoun. They are not interchangeable and cannot be joined by *and*.

Do not use a comma between cumulative adjectives.

The book talk featured three well-known English authors.

His résumé included various, short-term, landscaping jobs.

An exhibit of authentic, early Inca art was on display at the Royal Ontario Museum.

The music festival featured many Canadian, folk acts.

RESTRICTIVE AND NON-RESTRICTIVE ELEMENTS

Adjective clauses, adjective phrases, and appositives can modify nouns and pronouns. These modifying elements may be either restrictive or non-restrictive.

WHAT IS A RESTRICTIVE ELEMENT?

A **restrictive** element limits, defines, or identifies the noun or pronoun that it modifies. The information in a restrictive element is essential to a sentence's meaning. *Do not set off a restrictive element with commas.*

The man who has the scar above his left eyebrow is the chief robbery suspect.

WHAT IS A NON-RESTRICTIVE ELEMENT?

A **non-restrictive** element adds nonessential, or parenthetical, information about an idea or term that is already limited, defined, or identified; hence, a non-restrictive element is set off with a comma or commas.

The man who is the chief robbery subject has a scar, which is above his left eyebrow.

In some cases, however, you will need to know the context in which a sentence appears in order to decide whether a restrictive or non-restrictive element is required.

The man who is the chief robbery subject has a scar that is above his left eyebrow.

CONCLUDING ADVERB CLAUSES

Adverb clauses introducing a sentence almost always conclude with a comma. (See page 64.) However, when adverb clauses conclude a sentence and their meaning is essential to the sentence, they are not set off with commas. Adverb clauses that begin with the following subordinated conjunctions are usually essential:

after, as soon as, before, because, if, since, unless, until, when

Water boils at sea level, when it reaches a temperature of 100 degrees Celsius.

Place a comma before adverb clauses that contain non-essential information. Often, adverb clauses beginning with the following subordinating conjunctions are non-essential:

although, even though, though, whereas

He missed the turn for the expressway, even though signs for the on-ramp were prominently posted.

TRANSITIONS, PARENTHETICAL EXPRESSIONS, ABSOLUTE PHRASES, CONTRASTS

TRANSITIONAL EXPRESSIONS

Transitional expressions are words or groups of words that function as links between or within sentences. A transitional expression can appear at the beginning, end, or within a sentence. Examples of transitional expressions are conjunctive adverbs, such as *therefore* and *however*, and transitional phrases, such as *for example, in addition,* and *on the contrary*. (For a more complete list, see pages 71–72.)

If a transitional expression appears between independent clauses in a compound sentence, place a semicolon before it and, most often, a comma after the transitional expression.

Edwin did not fit in with our crowd; furthermore, he was openly antagonistic toward us.

The soprano was a prima donna; for instance, she demanded that mineral water chilled to a specific temperature be available in her dressing room before and after a performance.

Set off a transitional expression with commas if it appears at the start of a sentence or in the middle of an independent clause.

As a result, the medical insurance plan will not pay for liposuction.

The dermatologist comes highly recommended; he can't give me an appointment, however, until the end of March.

In some cases, if the transitional expression is integrated with the sentence and requires no pause or a minimal one when being read, no commas are needed to set off the expression. Expressions such as the following may not always need to be set off with commas:

at least, certainly, consequently, indeed, of course, perhaps, then, therefore, undoubtedly

You have been a good child; therefore you will get a pet pony.

Kenneth Thomson owns countless businesses; he is indeed a captain of Canadian industry.

PARENTHETICAL EXPRESSIONS

Parenthetical expressions contain additional information that the writer inserts into the sentence to explain, qualify, or give his or her point of view. If parenthetical expressions do not appear in parentheses, they are set off with commas.

The inarticulate politician, unfortunately, stated his contradictory views about abortion on national television.

In most writing situations, such as this one, commas are used to set off parenthetical expressions.

While commas are required to set off distinctly parenthetical expressions, *do not use commas to set off mildly parenthetical expressions.*

Team Canada, finally, scored the winning goal.

ABSOLUTE PHRASES

An absolute phrase contains a noun subject and a participle that modify an entire sentence. Set off absolute phrases with commas.

The war being over, the refugees returned home.

Their profits steeply declining, many computer companies laid off employees.

EXPRESSIONS OF CONTRAST

Expressions of contrast include words such as *not, nor, but,* or *unlike.* Set off expressions of contrast with commas.

The Toronto Raptors, unlike the Vancouver Grizzlies, flourished in Canada.

Martin found fame as a standup comedian, not as a writer.

NOUNS OF DIRECT ADDRESS, *YES* AND *NO*, INTERROGATIVE TAGS, INTERJECTIONS

Use commas to set off the following:

- nouns of direct address

    Your back flip, Olga, is of Olympic calibre.

- the words *yes* and *no*

    No, you can not rappel down the face of the university administration tower.

- interrogative tags

    You did turn off the iron, didn't you?

- mild interjections

    Then, incidents like that are inevitable.

HE SAID, ETC.

Use commas with speech tags such as *she said* or *he said* to set off direct quotations. (See also pages 80–82.)

Woody Allen wrote, "It is impossible to experience one's death objectively and still carry a tune."

"Defining and analyzing humor is a pastime of humorless people," said Robert Benchley.

DATES, ADDRESSES, TITLES, NUMBERS

DATES

When the date is within the sentence, use commas after the day and the year in month-day-year dates.

On August 14, 1945, Japan surrendered.

When the date is inverted or when only the month and year are given, commas are not required.

The birthday is celebrated on 24 May 2002.

January 2002 was unseasonably warm.

ADDRESSES

Use a comma between the city and province or city and country. When a sentence continues on after the city and province or city and country, use a comma after the province or country also.

Stephen Leacock died in Toronto, Ontario, in 1944.

In a complete address, separate all items except the postal code.

I would appreciate it if you would courier the book to Ennis James at 126 Mayfield Drive, Oakville, Ontario L6H 1K7.

TITLES

When an abbreviated title follows a name, place a comma after the name and a second comma after the title.

Philip Bacho, Ph.D., taught the course on writing scripts.

NUMBERS

Canada follows the international system of metric measurement, which does not use commas in numbers. Instead, spaces are used to separate sets of three digits. Four-digit numbers may be grouped together.

In your reading, you may encounter commas used after every three digits to the right for numbers that are four digits or more. This system was used before Canada adopted the international metric system.

4673 233 971 6 299, 381

Never use commas to separate sets of digits in years, telephone numbers, street numbers, or postal codes.

TO PREVENT CONFUSION

In many writing situations, commas are required to prevent reader confusion.

OMITTED WORDS

A comma is used to indicate that an understood word or words have been omitted.

Edwin adored jazz; Bert, gospel.

ECHOING WORDS

When two words repeat or strongly echo each other, a comma helps to clarify sentence meaning.

Undeterred by the possibility of plane hijackings, he felt that whatever happens, happens.

CLARIFYING A WRITER'S INTENTION

Occasionally commas are required to help readers group units of meaning as the writer intended.

> Those who can, run every chance they get.

The Semicolon

A semicolon is used to separate major elements of a sentence that are of equal grammatical rank.

INDEPENDENT CLAUSES WITH NO COORDINATING CONJUNCTION

An independent clause expresses a complete thought and can stand on its own as a sentence. When related independent clauses appear in a sentence (as in a compound sentence), they are usually linked by a comma and a coordinating conjunction (*and, but, for, nor, or, so,* and *yet*). The conjunction indicates the relationship between the clauses.

When the relationship between independent clauses is clear without the conjunction, you may instead link the two clauses with a semicolon.

> A teacher affects eternity; no one can tell where his influence stops.
>
> —*Henry Adams*

Use a semicolon if a coordinating conjunction between two independent clauses has been omitted. If you use a comma, you will create a grammatical error known as a comma splice.

> Provincial health insurance plans cover some medical costs when Canadians travel outside the country; they do not cover many vital health-care expenses.

Strategies for revising comma splice errors can be found on pages 8–10. You may wish to consider other alternatives to using a semicolon.

INDEPENDENT CLAUSES WITH TRANSITIONAL EXPRESSIONS

Transitional expressions can be conjunctive adverbs or transitional phrases.

Common Conjunctive Adverbs

accordingly, also, anyway, besides, certainly, consequently, conversely, finally, further, furthermore, hence, however, incidentally, indeed, instead, likewise, meanwhile, moreover, namely, nevertheless, next, nonetheless, now, otherwise, similarly, specifically, still, subsequently, then, thereafter, therefore, thus, undoubtedly

Transitional Phrases

after all, as a matter of fact, as an illustration, as a result, at any rate, at the same time, equally important, even so, for example, for instance, in addition, in conclusion, in fact, in other words, in short, in spite of, in summary, in the first place, in the same way, of course, on the contrary, on the other hand, to be sure, to illustrate

When a transitional expression comes between independent clauses, place a semicolon before the expression and a comma after it.

> She is an authority on the West Nile virus; furthermore, we need someone with her expertise.

If the transitional expression is in the middle of or at the end of the second independent clause, the semicolon is placed between the independent clauses.

> Generally people who work at the biological station have advanced postsecondary degrees; Tony, on the other hand, acquired his knowledge and expertise through practical experience.

Do not confuse the punctuation for transitional expressions with that used with coordinating conjunctions (*and*, *but*, *for*, *nor*, *or*, *so*, and *yet*). When a coordinating conjunction links two independent clauses, it is preceded by a comma. (See pages 8 and 64.)

SERIES WITH INTERNAL PUNCTUATION

Usually, commas separate items in a series. However, when series items contain commas, a semicolon is placed between items to make the sentence easier to read.

> The original cast of *Six Degrees of Separation* included Ouisa, Stockard Channing; Flan, John Cunningham; Geoffrey, Sam Stoneburner; and Paul, James McDaniel.

INCORRECT USES OF THE SEMICOLON

Never use a semicolon in the following writing situations:

- between independent clauses joined by *and*, *but*, *for*, *nor*, *or*, *so*, or *yet*

> lifetime, yet
>
> The painter was very prolific during his ~~lifetime; yet~~ he achieved the fame he deserved only after death.

- between a subordinate clause and the remainder of the sentence

  After she made the lemon curd; Leona whipped the cream she needed to frost the cake.

- between an appositive and the word to which it refers

  Raj's favourite television program is *Six Feet Under*; a dark but funny dramatic series.

- to introduce a list

  A number of great novels are covered in the course; *Bleak House, Pride and Prejudice*, and *Gulliver's Travels*.

The Colon

The colon is used most often to indicate a formal, emphatic introductory word, phrase, or clause that follows it.

BEFORE A LIST, AN APPOSITIVE, A QUOTATION

Use a colon before

- a list

  For this experiment, you will need the following materials: three clear, colourless liquids in numbered cups; a transparent sheet; a waterproof marker; an eyedropper or a small measuring spoon; and paper towels.

- an appositive

  While held hostage, the journalist had one all-consuming thought: survival.

- a quotation

  Mackenzie King summed up his position in the motto: "Not necessarily conscription, but conscription if necessary."

For additional ways of introducing quotations, see pages 81–82.

BETWEEN INDEPENDENT CLAUSES

In North America, there are two classes of travel: there is first-class travel, and then there is travel with children.

You can use a capital letter or a lowercase letter to begin the independent clause after the colon.

CONVENTIONAL USES

The colon is conventionally used

- after the salutation of a formal letter

  Dear Ms. Pointman:

- to indicate hours and minutes

  6:31 a.m. (or A.M.)

- between numbers in ratios

  The ratio of men over fifty was 5:1.

- between the title and subtitle of a book

  Dancing at the Edge of the World: Thoughts on Words, Women, Places

- to separate the city from the publisher and date in a bibliographic entry

  Toronto: Nelson, 2003.

- between Bible chapters and verses

  Psalms 23:1–3

INCORRECT USES OF THE COLON

Except in documentation, a complete independent clause must precede a colon.

Do not use a colon in the following writing situations:

- between a verb and its complement or object

  The main ingredients in a good mushroom omelet are: eggs, mushrooms, and butter.

- between a preposition and its object

  The open-area portion of the dome house consisted of: a kitchen, living room, and master bedroom.

- after *for example, such as,* and *including/included*

  The content of the botanist's lecture included: boreal forests, a Carolinian forest, and an Amazonian rain forest.

The Apostrophe

POSSESSIVE NOUNS

An apostrophe (') appears as part of a noun to indicate that the word is possessive. Often ownership is obvious, as in

Mishka's hockey stick or *the instructor's briefcase*. Sometimes ownership is not as explicit, as in *the journey's end* or *the river's tributaries*. To determine whether a noun is possessive, see if you can state it as an *of* phrase, as in *the end of the journey* or *the tributaries of the river*. In these examples, both nouns, *journey's* and *river's*, are possessive.

ADD -'S IF

1. The noun does not end in -s.

   The commodore's cabin cruiser.

   It was the team's wish that the donation be made in his name.

2. The noun is singular and ends in -s.

   Gus's father owns a single-engine plane.

Exception: An apostrophe without an -s may be added to a singular noun if adding another -s would make the word difficult to pronounce.

Moses' mountain journey is an important part of his legacy.

In such instances, it is acceptable to write the word with just the apostrophe or with an apostrophe and -s.

ADD ONLY AN APOSTROPHE IF

The noun is plural and ends in -s.

Workers' rights were neglected by the military regime.

WITH COMPOUND SUBJECTS

With a compound subject, use -'s (or -s') with the last noun only to show joint possession.

You should see Doug and Dino's modified stock car.

Make all nouns possessive to show individual possession.

Todd's and Margaret's ideas on how to decorate the home were diametrically opposed.

WITH COMPOUND NOUNS

Use -'s (or -s') with the last element in a compound noun to show possession.

My sister-in-law's film won a Genie.

POSSESSIVE INDEFINITE PRONOUNS

An indefinite pronoun refers to a general or nonspecific person or thing. Examples of indefinite pronouns are *somebody, anything*, and *anyone*. Add -'s to the end of the indefinite pronoun to make it possessive.

It is not anybody's business what I do in my free time.

Someone's laptop was stolen from the reference library.

CONTRACTIONS

The apostrophe takes the place of missing letters in contractions.

Who's going to do it doesn't matter.

The apostrophe can also indicate that the first two digits of years have been left out.

There will be a reunion for the class of '88.

Did you enjoy *That '70s* Show?

However, -s without an apostrophe is added to years in a decade.

She lived in Paris in the 1940s.

PLURALS OF NUMBERS, LETTERS, ETC.

Other common writing situations where -'s is used to pluralize include

- numbers

  As scores for his perfect dive, he received all 10's.

- letters

  The living rooms in the condominium all formed *L*'s.

- words as words

  I don't want to have to deal with any more *what if*'s.

Notice that -s is not italicized when used with italicized words or letters.

- abbreviations

  Each of the M.P.'s was assigned to a committee.

According to the Modern Language Association, however, no apostrophe is needed with plurals of numbers and abbreviations.

He has trouble writing 6s.

I bought some new DVDs.

INCORRECT USES OF THE APOSTROPHE

Do not use an apostrophe with

- nouns that are not possessive

The clients' had expected us to pick up the tab for dinner.

- the possessive pronouns *his, hers, its, ours, theirs,* and *whose*

That is it's first time out of the box.

Here, *its* is the possessive form. *It's* is the contraction for *it is*.

Quotation Marks

DIRECT QUOTATIONS

Direct quotations are the exact words copied from a print source or transcribed from what a person says. Direct quotations must be enclosed within quotation marks.

"The open ocean is normally a friendly environment for a sea kayak," writes John Dowd in *Sea Kayaking: A Manual for Long-Distance Touring*.

On the other hand, indirect quotations paraphrase or summarize what has appeared in a print source or what a person has said. Indirect quotations are not placed within quotation marks.

John Dowd professes that generally the open ocean is a safe place to sea kayak.

QUOTING LONGER PASSAGES BY A SINGLE SPEAKER

If you are directly quoting passages by a single speaker, start each new paragraph with quotation marks, but do not use closing quotation marks until the end of the quoted material.

MARKING A CHANGE IN SPEAKER WITHIN DIALOGUE

Start a new paragraph to signal a change in the speaker.

"I said me, not you."
"Oh. You got a car outside?"
"I can walk."

"That's five miles back to where the van is."
"People have walked five miles."

—*Alice Munro, "Friend of My Youth"*

LONG QUOTATIONS

PROSE

A "long" quotation of prose is any passage that is more than four typed or handwritten lines. Indent the entire quotation ten spaces from the left margin. You do not need to enclose the longer quotation within quotation marks because the indented format establishes for the reader that the quotation is taken exactly from a source. Usually, longer quotations are introduced by a sentence ending with a colon.

> Smoking can destroy the health of smokers and is a very real health risk to those around them, as researcher Warren Clark clearly points out:
>
> > In 1995, 4.5 million nonsmoking Canadians aged 15 and over were exposed to cigarette smoke on a daily basis. Another 2.2 million were exposed to it at least once a week, while about 840 000 were exposed to it less frequently. In terms of percentages, about 28 per cent of nonsmokers aged 15 and over breathed secondhand smoke every day, while about 19 per cent were exposed to it somewhat less often. Just over half of nonsmokers reported that they were not exposed to ETS (environmental tobacco smoke) (161).

Placing the page number within parentheses follows the citation style prescribed by the Modern Language Association. (See page 101.)

If the direct quotation had included additional paragraphs, the first line of each new paragraph would need to be indented an additional three spaces.

POETRY

A "long" quotation of poetry is more than three lines of the poem. Indent the quotation ten spaces from the left margin. You do not need to enclose the longer quotation within quotation marks because the indented format establishes for the reader that the quotation is taken exactly from the poem. Use quotation marks within the quotation only if they are part of the poem. (For information on how to punctuate two or three lines of poetry, see page 88.)

> P.K. Page is more personal in "After Rain" than in "The Stenographers." She defines her own poetic sensibility through the poem-within-a-poem of stanza three:

the clothes-reel gauche
as the rangy skeleton of some
gaunt delicate spidery mute
is pitched as if
listening;
while hung from one thin rib
a silver web
its infant, skeletal, diminutive,
now sagged with sequins, pulled ellipsoid,
glistening.

If your paper is written according to the style of the American Psychological Association, you will need to follow slightly different guidelines for setting off long quotations (see page 123).

QUOTATIONS WITHIN QUOTATIONS

Single quotation marks enclose quotations within quotations.

According to Newman et al., Charles de Gaulle "spoke the words that jolted a nation: 'Vive le Québec libre!' "

Two different quotation marks appear at the end of the quotation. The single quotation mark completes the interior quotation, while the double quotation mark completes the main quotation.

TITLES

Use quotation marks around titles of works that are included within other works, such as poems, short stories, newspaper and magazine articles, radio programs, television episodes, and chapters and other subdivisions of books.

His talk focused on point of view in Edgar Allan Poe's short story "The Tell-Tale Heart."

The titles of plays, books, and films and the names of magazines appear in italics if you are typing your manuscript. They are underlined if your manuscript is handwritten.

WORDS AS WORDS

Italics or underlining is preferred for setting off words used as words. However, it is acceptable to use quotation marks for this purpose.

I remember once displaying my ignorance by using the word *irregardless* when I should have used *regardless*.

I remember once displaying my ignorance by using the word "irregardless" when I should have used "regardless."

WITH OTHER PUNCTUATION

The following section provides rules for using punctuation with quotation marks.

COMMAS AND PERIODS
Place commas and periods inside quotation marks.

> "I'm not finished yet," she said. "The books I looked at were of no help."

Also follow the above punctuation rule in the following cases:

1. with single quotation marks
2. for titles of works
3. for words used as words

Exception: If you follow Modern Language Association style guidelines for your paper, the period follows the final parenthesis in parenthetical in-text citations. In this case, the period is outside the quotation marks.

> Clarkson and McCall contend "Davis was apprehensive that Trudeau's pugnacity might scupper the possibility" (368).

SEMICOLONS AND COLONS
Place semicolons and colons outside quotation marks.

> He explained his term "in the moment": the individual focuses himself or herself on the elusive present.

> As the bank's head economist, she asserts that the economy will soon "take off"; several of her colleagues at other banks strongly disagree.

QUESTION MARKS AND EXCLAMATION POINTS
If the question mark or exclamation point is part of the quoted material, place the question mark or exclamation point *inside* the quotation marks.

> *Part of the Quoted Material*
> When Jeff heard what Susan had done, he shouted, "She made the shot from centre court!"

If the question mark or exclamation point applies to the entire sentence, place the question mark or exclamation point *outside* the quotation marks.

> *Applies to the Entire Sentence*
> What do you think of Napoleon's view that "history is a set of lies agreed upon"?

According to MLA style, the question mark or exclamation point is placed before the final closing quotation mark; a sentence period is then placed after the final parenthesis in the parenthetical citation.

> Oliver Sacks ponders, "If this was the case in Virgil, what might happen if visual function was suddenly made possible, demanded?" (291).

INTRODUCING QUOTED MATERIAL

You have three major punctuation options when using a group of words to introduce a quotation:

1. a colon
2. a comma
3. no punctuation

WHEN TO USE THE COLON

Use the colon if the quotation has been formally introduced. A formal introduction is a complete independent clause.

> In *The Globe and Mail*, John Stackhouse presents the following insight about political change in Africa: "The economic revolution that has swept through Africa, from the highlands of eastern Kenya to the rain forests of Ivory Coast, has affected almost every African—and altered few governments."

WHEN TO USE THE COMMA

Use a comma if a quotation is introduced with or followed by an expression such as *she said* or *he uttered*.

> Giving fresh meaning to a cliché, the smoke jumper said, "Where there's smoke, there's fire."

> "I'm a Canadian," I protested.

WHEN A QUOTATION IS BLENDED INTO A SENTENCE

Use a comma or no punctuation, depending on how the quotation fits into the grammatical structure of the sentence.

> She walked with an awkward jerky gait, as though she were not at home on her own legs, and as she passed by, the other kids would whisper, "Pigeon-Toed Cochran!"

> In summertime, all expeditions were planned tentatively; sentences ended with the phrase "if it doesn't rain."

WHEN A QUOTATION BEGINS A SENTENCE

Use a comma to set off a quotation at the beginning of a sentence.

"I'll be back in a moment," I told my students, and half out of my mind with anxiety, I went down in the lift, dashed across the street, and burst into Adriana's house.

However, a comma is not needed if the opening quotation ends with a question mark or an exclamation point.

"What are you doing?" I demanded.

WHEN A QUOTED SENTENCE IS INTERRUPTED BY EXPLANATORY WORDS

Use commas to set off the explanatory words.

"No," he called back, "I can see it breathing!"

WHEN TWO SUCCESSIVE QUOTED SENTENCES ARE INTERRUPTED BY EXPLANATORY WORDS

Use a comma before the explanatory words within the quotation marks of the first quotation. End the explanatory words with a period.

"We are simply not well prepared for the rapid development that we have been experiencing," Dr. Muangman said. "Politicians and decision makers think that if we make a lot of money, that is enough."

INCORRECT USES OF QUOTATION MARKS

Do not use quotation marks around indirect quotations.

My mother always said longingly that she'd "like to visit Greece."

Do not use quotation marks to call attention to a word or expression. Never use quotation marks to distance yourself from an expression or to call attention to slang.

Some might say the mechanic went on a "busman's holiday."

Do not use quotation marks to set off your own essay title.

Other Marks

PERIOD

Periods are commonly used to indicate the end of a sentence and within abbreviations.

ENDING SENTENCES

Use the period after statements, indirect questions, and mild commands.

Statement

Use a period after a statement.

> Rock climbing on the Bruce Trail can be dangerous.

Indirect Question

After a direct question, use a question mark.

> Do you want to walk the Gun Point Loop section of the trail?

However, if the question is **indirect**, use a period to end the sentence.

> The hike leader inquired if they wanted to walk the Gun Point Loop section of the trail.

Mild Command

After a strong command, use the exclamation point.

> Please, call an ambulance now!

However, after a **mild command**—an imperative or declarative sentence that is not an exclamation—use a period.

> Please pick up the groceries.

ABBREVIATIONS

Use periods in abbreviations such as the following:

a.m. (or A.M.)	p.	B.A.	Dr.	Inc.
p.m. (or P.M.)	etc.	M.A.	Ms.	Ltd.
B.C. (or B.C.E.)	e.g.	M.B.A.	Mrs.	Dec.
A.D. (or C.E.)	i.e.	Ph.D.	Mr.	St.

Do not use periods with Canada Post abbreviations, such as SK, ON, and NB.

Widely recognized abbreviations for organizations, companies, and countries do not require periods, although periods are often used in U.K. and U.S.

> CBC CSIS NFB UK US IBM UN NBA CFL

If you are in doubt about whether an abbreviation requires a period, check in a good Canadian dictionary or encyclopedia. To check the abbreviation of a name of a company, you might consult that company's website.

Do not add a second period if the sentence ends with an abbreviation's period.

He always wanted to complete his M.A.

QUESTION MARK

FOLLOWING A DIRECT QUESTION

Use a question mark after any direct questions.

Are you coming or going?

Also use a question mark after a polite request.

Would you please forward to me a copy of the article for my files?

Use a period after an indirect question.

Selby asked if she could go home.

FOLLOWING QUESTIONS IN A SERIES THAT ARE NOT COMPLETE SENTENCES

Use a question mark to end each question in a series, even if series questions are not complete sentences.

We are curious to hear what Justin's career goal will be this week. Maybe a brain surgeon? Perhaps a stockbroker? Or maybe a travel agent?

EXCLAMATION POINT

Use the exclamation point with an emphatic declaration or a strong command.

The plane will hit the mountain!

Get out of the way, quickly!

Do not over-use the exclamation point.

Over-use: We climbed the mountain on Hornby and had an incredible view! On one side was the snowcapped Coastal Range! On the other side, we could see majestic Mount Washington!

Correction: We climbed the mountain on Hornby and had an incredible view. On one side was the snowcapped Coastal Range. On the other side, we could see majestic Mount Washington.

DASH

The dash marks a strong break in the continuity of a sentence. It can be used to add information, emphasize part of a sentence, or set off part of the sentence for clarity.

To make a dash using your computer, enter two unspaced hyphens (--). Do not leave a space before the first hyphen or after the second hyphen. Many computer programs automatically format dashes when you enter two consecutive hyphens. Another option is to use the "Insert/Symbol" feature in your software.

Use dashes to

- enclose a sentence element that interrupts the flow of thought, or to set off parenthetical material that deserves emphasis

  Our civilization is decadent and our language—so the argument runs—must inevitably share in the general collapse.
  —*George Orwell, "Politics and the English Language"*

- set off appositives that contain commas

  Teachers—those educators, parents, entertainers, baby sitters, and counsellors—are undervalued and underpaid by society.

- show a dramatic shift in tone or thought

  At the NBA All-Star Game, Michael Jordan took the pass, eluded the defender, hit full stride, soared—and missed an uncontested dunk.

- restate

  Although they are close together—living only a few kilometres apart—they may as well be on different sides of the planet.

- amplify

  Peanut butter was everywhere—in their hair, on their clothes, smudged on their glasses.

- prepare a list

  In the storage room are all the paint supplies—paints, paint thinner, canvas covering sheets, brushes, rollers, and roller trays.

Do not over-use dashes. If over-used, dashes can lose their effectiveness and make writing disjointed. The Modern Language Association manual suggests limiting the number of dashes in a sentence to two paired dashes or one unpaired dash.

Over-use: Three students—Anwar, Sanjah, and Pete—won prizes—scholarships, books, and medallions. This is quite an achievement—especially for Pete since he studies only minimally—if at all.

Correction: Three students—Anwar, Sanjah, and Pete—won prizes, which included scholarships, books, and medallions. This is quite an achievement, especially for Pete, since he studies only minimally, if at all.

PARENTHESES

Parentheses are used to set off helpful, non-essential, additional information. While dashes usually call attention to the information they enclose, parentheses often de-emphasize the information they enclose.

Use parentheses to

- enclose supplemental information, such as definitions, examples, digressions or asides, and contrasts

  Calgary is fourth among cities in Canada for number of head offices located within its city limits (280 in 2002).

  Kenner taught at Assumption College (now University of Windsor), 1946–48, and was a long-time professor of English and Chair at the University of California at Santa Barbara, 1950–73.

- enclose letters or numbers that label items in a series

  Follow these directions to make a puppet: (1) draw and cut out a head for your puppet, (2) link three or four paper clips together, and (3) attach a string to the head of the puppet and tape the string to a stiff piece of paper, such as a notebook cover.

Do not over-use parentheses. Including too much parenthetical information can make your writing seem choppy and awkward. Often you can integrate information from parentheses into your sentences so they flow smoothly.

The second phase of railway building in Canada ~~(starting 1867)~~ came with Confederation. in 1867

BRACKETS

Brackets are used to enclose any words you insert into quoted material. You may need to add or change a word so that a quotation will fit smoothly into the structure of your essay sentences, or to clarify information or ideas for readers. As well, brackets are used to indicate an error in the original quoted material.

TO ADD OR SUBSTITUTE CLARIFYING INFORMATION IN A QUOTATION

> "I rode swiftly toward Sitting Bull's camp. Then I saw the white soldiers fighting in line [Reno's men]."

TO INDICATE ERRORS IN ORIGINAL MATERIAL

The Latin word *sic* means "so" or "thus." The word *sic* is placed in brackets immediately after a word in a quotation that appears erroneous or odd. *Sic* indicates that the word is quoted exactly as it stands in the original.

> "Growing up on the small island [sic] of Nanaimo, British Columbia, Diana Krall has made a name for herself as a jazz singer."

ELLIPSIS MARK

An ellipsis mark consists of three spaced periods (. . .). The ellipsis is used to indicate that you have omitted material from the original writer's quoted words.

WHEN DELETING MATERIAL FROM A QUOTATION

> Gagnon states that "as much as 65% to 70% of semen volume originates from the seminal vesicles . . . and about 5% from the minor sexual glands."

An ellipsis is not required at the beginning of a quotation. Do not place an ellipsis at the end of the quotation unless you have omitted content from the final quoted sentence.

WHEN DELETING A FULL SENTENCE FROM THE MIDDLE OF A QUOTED PASSAGE

Use a period before the three ellipsis points if you need to delete a full sentence or more from the middle of a quoted passage.

> Priestly's ideas on nationalism are not flattering. He says, "If we deduct from nationalism all that is borrowed or stolen from regionalism, what remains is mostly rubbish. . . . Almost all nationalist movements are led by ambitious, frustrated men determined to hold office."

WHEN QUOTING POETRY

Use a full line of spaced dots to indicate that you have omitted one or more lines from the quotation of a poem.

Death, be not proud, though some have called thee
Mighty and dreadful, for thou art not so;

. . . .

From rest and sleep, which but thy pictures be,
Much pleasure; then from thee much more must flow,

—*John Donne,* Holy Sonnets

WHEN INDICATING INTERRUPTION OR HESITATION IN SPEECH OR THOUGHT

Often in story dialogue or narration, an ellipsis is used to indicate hesitation or interruption in speech or thought.

"Well . . . I couldn't make it. I didn't get to the exam."

SLASH

USING SLASHES TO INDICATE LINES OF POETRY

The slash is used most often in academic writing to indicate the ends of lines of poetry when these have been incorporated into the essay text. Up to two or three lines from a poem can be quoted.

Atwood's "Death of a Young Son by Drowning" opens with the haunting lines, "He, who navigated with success / the dangerous river of his own birth / once more set forth."

Leave one space before and one space after the slash. For quoted passages of poetry that are four or more lines in length, start each line of the poem on its own line, indented in the style of block quotations.

USING THE SLASH TO INDICATE OPTIONS OR PAIRED ITEMS

Sometimes the slash is used between options or paired items. Examples include *actor/producer, life/death, pass/fail.* In these cases, do not leave a space before and after the slash.

Since the orchestra was short of funds, he served as artistic director/conductor.

Avoid the use of *he/she, his/her*, and *and/or* because they are informal and awkward in writing.

MECHANICS

MECHANICS

The mechanical details of a document often have a great deal to do with creating a good first impression on your reader. Care and consistency with details will help to ensure your credibility as a writer. Little things mean a lot.

Capitalization

Capitalize the first word of every sentence. In addtion, you will need to capitalize specific types of words within sentences. Use the following rules as general guidelines for capitalization. Consult your dictionary to determine which words must be capitalized.

PROPER VS. COMMON NOUNS

Capitalize proper nouns and words derived from them, but do not capitalize common nouns. Proper nouns are the names of people, places, and some things. Common nouns are all other nouns.

As a general rule, capitalize the following:

- names of religions, religious practitioners, holy books, special religious days, and deities
- geographic place names
- people's names and nicknames
- words of family relationship used as names (e.g., Uncle Bill)
- nationalities, tribes, races, and languages
- names of historical events, periods, movements, documents, and treaties
- political parties, organizations, and government departments
- educational institutions, departments, degrees, and specific courses
- names of celestial bodies
- names of ships, planes, and aircraft
- parts of letters (e.g., Dear John)
- names of specific software progress

Months, days of the week, and holidays are considered proper nouns. The seasons and numbers of days of the month are not considered proper nouns.

Every spring, Victoria Day falls on a Monday in May.

The meeting is held on the second Tuesday of January, June, and December.

Capitalize the names of school subjects only if they are languages, but capitalize the names of specific courses.

CAPITALIZING NOUNS

PROPER NOUNS	COMMON NOUNS
Zeus	a god
Book of Mormon	a book
Kamloops	a city
Marcel	a man
Aunt Agnes	my aunt
Portuguese	a language
Romanticism	a movement
New Democratic Party	a political party
Mars	a planet
Queen Elizabeth II	a ship
Microsoft Word	a software program

In his final year, he will need to take microbiology, chemistry, biology, English, and Spanish.

Professor Woodman teaches Romanticism to all students majoring in English.

TITLES WITH PROPER NAMES

Capitalize the title of a person when it is part of a proper name.

Dr. Norman Bethune   Rev. David Rooke

Pat McLauglin, P.Eng.   Douglas Fairbanks, Sr.

Judge Shepperd gave his decision on the appeal.

Do not capitalize the title when it is used alone.

A judge presided over the inquiry.

Note: In some cases, if the title of an important public figure is used alone, the first letter can appear as either a capital letter or a lowercase letter. Conventions vary.

The <u>prime minister</u> [Prime Minister] dodged the protester's pie.

TITLES OF WORKS

Capitalize the first, last, and all other important words in the titles of works such as books, articles, films, and songs.

IMPORTANT WORDS

These important words should be capitalized in titles and subtitles:

- nouns
- verbs
- adjectives
- adverbs

LESS IMPORTANT WORDS

These less important words should not be capitalized *unless* they are the first or last word of the title or subtitle:

- articles
- prepositions
- coordinating conjunctions

Book Title: *A Feminist Dictionary*

Article Title: "A Turkey with Taste"

Film Title: *From Earth to the Moon*

Song Title: "Do You Know the Way to San José?"

Use the same guidelines to capitalize chapter titles and other major divisions in a work.

"Phantom of the Canadian Opera: Trudeau's Revenge" is Chapter 11 in Peter C. Newman's *The Canadian Revolution*.

FIRST WORD OF A SENTENCE

Capitalize the first word of a sentence.

It's Monday morning, time for the weekly editorial meeting at a mass-market publishing house.

If a sentence appears within parentheses, capitalize the first word of the sentence. However, do not capitalize the first word if the parentheses are within another sentence.

The effects of plaque on the heart valves are significant. (<u>See</u> Figure 6.)

The effects of plaque on the heart valves are significant (see Figure 6).

FIRST WORD OF A QUOTED SENTENCE

Capitalize the first word of a direct quotation, but do not capitalize it if the quotation is blended into the sentence in which the quotation is introduced.

> The department chair defended the embattled professor, arguing, "He is an outstanding teacher and the evidence against him is flimsy at best."

> In his article "Eco-tourism Boom: How Much Can Wildlife Take?" Bruce Obee says that "tour boats . . . are a fraction of the traffic."

If you need to interrupt a quoted sentence to include explanatory words, do not capitalize the first word following the interruption.

> "She goes by bus," the mother exclaimed with anger, "and I'm not very happy about that."

If you need to quote poetry in an essay, use the capitalization employed by the poet.

> Season of mists and mellow fruitfulness,
> Close bosom-friend of the maturing sun;
> Conspiring with him how to load and bless
> With fruit the vines that round the thatch-eves run; . . .
> —*John Keats, "To Autumn"*

Many modern poets do not follow the conventions of capitalization. When quoting their work, copy the text exactly.

> so much depends
> upon
> a red wheel
> barrow
> —*William Carlos Williams, "The Red Wheelbarrow"*

FIRST WORD AFTER A COLON

When an independent clause appears after a colon, capitalizing the first word is optional; if the content after the colon is not an independent clause, do not capitalize.

> We were told to bring the following items for the hike: a compass, a sleeping bag, a tent, and enough food to last seven days.

There is one major reason that Phillip doesn't want Kathleen for a friend: He doesn't trust her.

ABBREVIATIONS

Capitalize the abbreviations for government departments and agencies, names of organizations and corporations, trade names, and call letters of television and radio stations.

CSIS CIA NATO CTV Magna International CHCO-TV CKNW

Abbreviations

In most cases, abbreviations should not be used in formal writing, such as academic essays, unless the abbreviations are very well known, such as *CBC* or *UN*. Abbreviations are more widely used in science and technical writing than in writing for the humanities.

Always consider your reader when deciding whether to use any abbreviation. Will he or she understand the abbreviation? If not, you run the risk of frustrating the reader. If the type of writing that you are doing requires abbreviations, be consistent in your use of them.

TITLES WITH PROPER NAMES

Abbreviate titles and degrees immediately before and after proper names.

Do not abbreviate a title or degree if it does not accompany a proper name.

reverend
The ~~rev.~~ gave a very inspiring sermon to launch the congregation's food drive.

Do not use titles and degrees redundantly:

Dr. Steven Edwards, M.D.

Instead use one of these options:

Dr. Steven Edwards

Steven Edwards, M.D.

ORGANIZATIONS, CORPORATIONS, AND COUNTRIES

Use standard abbreviations for names of countries, organizations, and corporations.

UK (or U.K.) FBI NORAD RCMP CIDA TSN RCA IBM

To save money, she got a room at the YWCA.

ABBREVIATED TITLES	
BEFORE PROPER NAMES	AFTER PROPER NAMES
Rev. R. W. McLean	Edward Zenker, D.V.D.
Dr. Wendy Wong	Paul Martin, Jr.
Asst. Prof. Tom Simpson	Margaret Barcza, M.B.A.
Ms. Germaine Greer	John Bruner, LL.D.
Mrs. Sodha Singh	Eleanor Semple, D.D.
Mr. Wil Loman	Roy Shoicket, M.D.
St. John	Barbara Zapert, Ph.D.

If you need to use a less familiar abbreviation in your paper, such as *COMECON* for the Council of Mutual Economic Assistance, do the following:

1. Write the full name of the organization followed by the abbreviation in parentheses.
2. For each subsequent reference to the organization, use the abbreviation on its own.

B.C., A.D., a.m., p.m., no., $

Use the standard abbreviations *B.C.*, *A.D.*, *a.m.*, *p.m.*, *no.*, and $ only with particular years, times, numbers, or amounts.

The abbreviation *B.C.* ("before Christ") or the acceptable alternative *B.C.E.* ("before the Common Era") always appears after a specific date.

156 B.C. (or B.C.E.)

The abbreviation *A.D.* ("Anno Domini") or the acceptable alternative *C.E.* ("Common Era") always appears before a specific date.

A.D. (or C.E.) 65

Use *a.m.*, *p.m.*, *no.*, or $ only with a particular figure.

5:15 a.m. (or A.M.)   8:30 p.m. (or P.M.) $175   no. 16 (or No.)

In formal writing, do not use these abbreviations without particular figures.

afternoon.

We arrived for the dance in the early ~~p.m.~~

It is impossible to estimate the ~~no.~~ number of fish in the stream during spawning season.

LATIN ABBREVIATIONS

Some readers may be unfamiliar with Latin abbreviations, so keep use of these abbreviations to a minimum or use the English equivalent.

LATIN ABBREVIATIONS

ABBREVIATION	LATIN	ENGLISH MEANING
c.	*circa*	approximately
cf.	*confer*	compare
e.g.	*exempli gratia*	for example
et al.	*et alii*	and others
etc.	*et cetera*	and the rest
i.e.	*id est*	that is
N.B.	*nota bene*	note well
P.S.	*postscriptum*	postscript
vs.	*versus*	versus

In informal writing, such as personal e-mails, it is acceptable to use Latin abbreviations.

Jennifer wants to go the Canadiens game this Tuesday. It's the Canadiens vs. the Flames. After the game let's grab a burger, etc. N.B. Dominique and her gang will be there.

In formal writing, use the full English words or phrases.

The Sumerians came down to the bank of the Euphrates and Tigris rivers ~~c.~~ approximately 3500 B.C.E. Many artifacts provide evidence of their cultural advancement ~~e.g.~~ , for example, the bronze mask portrait of King Sargon and the headdress of Queen Shub-ad.

bbreviations are generally not appropriate in formal writing.

canadian literature

Margaret Atwood is a popular author in ~~Can. lit.~~ classes because she has written so many outstanding novels.

INFORMAL ABBREVIATIONS TO AVOID IN FORMAL WRITING

CATEGORY	FORMAL	INFORMAL
Names of persons	Jennifer	Jen
Holidays	Christmas	Xmas
Days of the week	Tuesday to Thursday	Tues. to Thurs.
Months	from January to August	Jan. to Aug.
Provinces and countries	Saskatchewan	Sask. or SK
Academic subjects	Biology and English	Bio. and Eng.
Units of measurement*	6 ounces	6 oz.
Addresses	Madison Avenue	Madison Ave.
Subdivisions of books	chapter, page	ch., p.**

* except metric measurements
** except as part of documentation

Metric abbreviations are often permitted in formal writing, as in 25 *kg* or 15 *mm*. However, do not use a number written in words with an abbreviation, as in *twenty cm*.

Abbreviations are acceptable in company or institution names only if the abbreviation is part the company's or institution's official name, as in *Jack's Windows & Roofing Co.*, or *Writer's Inc. Consulting*. Never arbitrarily abbreviate a company's name. For example, if a company's name is *Randolph Architectural Group*, do not shorten it to *Randolph Arch. Gr.* When corresponding with any company, use the full company name as it appears on the company stationery, or in the firm's advertising, or on its website.

DOCUMENTATION

DOCUMENTATION

When writing academic research papers, you must acknowledge information and ideas obtained from other sources. This includes information and ideas that you directly quote, summarize, or paraphrase from others' work.

There are numerous academic style guides, and each discipline follows a particular documentation style. The documentation styles differ in the way they cite sources and format citations.

This section provides an overview of essential guidelines in the *MLA Handbook for Writers of Research Papers* (6th ed., 2003), used primarily in the humanities; in the *Publication Manual of the American Psychological Association* (5th ed., 2001), used primarily in the social sciences; in *The Chicago Manual of Style* (15th ed., 2003); and in *Scientific Style and Format: The CBE* [Council of Biology Editors] *Manual for Authors, Editors, and Publishers* (6th ed., 1994).

MLA Style of Documentation

IN-TEXT CITATIONS: MLA STYLE

If a reader, such as your instructor, wants to check any source have you used for a direct quotation, summary, or paraphrase, he or she needs complete information to do so.

When following the MLA style, you document your sources in two ways:

1. within the body of the paper, using **in-text citations**
2. at the end of the paper, in a **list of works cited** (see page 106)

Documentation guidelines within this section are consistent with the MLA style described in *MLA Handbook for Writers of Research Papers*, 6th ed. (New York: MLA, 2003).

IN-TEXT PARENTHETICAL REFERENCES

An in-text citation consists of a parenthetical reference that gives the minimum information necessary to identify a source and locate the relevant material within it. This reference usually consists of the author's last name (unless the preceding text mentions the author's name) and a page number or numbers. Full information on the source is supplied in the list of works cited. A typical MLA Works Cited entry begins with the name of the author.

The MLA prefers to see parenthetical references used as infrequently as possible; for example, when citing an entire work, the author's name in the sentence, accompanied by the work's title if you wish, is often all that is required. Also in the interest of brevity, the MLA often uses abbreviations in parenthetical references and documentation.

Placement: Parenthetical references should be placed as close to the borrowed material as possible without interfering with readability, preferably at the end of the sentence.

Punctuation: Unless you are using a long quotation, the punctuation mark appears after the parenthetical citation. If the author's name is required within the parenthetical reference, no punctuation is required between the author's name and the page number.

Inclusive page numbers: When the information you are quoting or citing spans more than one page, always give inclusive page numbers, for example, 245–46. For page numbers 100 and up, give only the last two digits of the second number unless more are necessary, as in 1206–1316.

The remainder of this section provides models to illustrate the MLA citation style.

Author Mentioned in Preceding Text

When the author's name is provided in the preceding text, give only the page reference within the parentheses.

> Peter Schrag observes that America is "divided between affluence and poverty, between slums and suburbs" (118).

The sentence period appears after the parenthetical reference. For information about punctuating quotations that end in exclamation points or question marks, see pages 80–81.

Author Not Mentioned in Preceding Text

If the author's name is not provided in the preceding text, it must appear with the page reference within parentheses. No punctuation is required between the author's name and the page reference.

> One commentator notes that America is "divided between affluence and poverty, between slums and suburbs" (Schrag 118).

Two or More Works by the Same Author

When you use two or more works by the same author in a research paper, you will have a corresponding number of entries for that author in your list of works cited. Your in-text citation must direct the reader to the correct Works Cited entry. You can do this in one of three ways:

1. If you have provided the author's name and the title of the work in the preceding text, include only the page number(s) in parentheses.

   In Lament for a Nation, George Grant claims that "modern civilization makes all local cultures anachronistic" (54).

2. If only the author's name is given in the preceding text, include the title of the work in an abbreviated form within the parenthetical reference.

   George Grant claims that "modern civilization makes all local cultures anachronistic" (Lament 54).

3. If not mentioned in the preceding text, include the author's last name and the title of the work within the parenthetical reference. Use a comma to separate the author's name and the title.

   Some propose that "modern civilization makes all local cultures anachronistic" (Grant, Lament 54).

As in the above examples, the book title should be underlined or appear in italics. (MLA prefers underlining in material that will be graded; check your instructor's preference.) If the cited work is an article, its title should be placed within quotation marks.

Two or Three Authors

You can include the names of the authors in the text or place them in a parenthetical reference.

> According to Clarkson and McCall, even late in the decade of the Quiet Revolution, "Trudeau saw the constitutional question as only one facet of his general mandate for the Justice Department" (258).

> Even late in the decade of the Quiet Revolution, "Trudeau saw the constitutional question as only one facet of his general mandate for the Justice Department" (Clarkson and McCall 258).

With three authors, use a serial comma in the reference: (Wynkin, Blynkin, and Nodd viii).

More Than Three Authors

If the work you are citing has more than three authors, you could name all of the authors, using serial commas, or you could include only the last name of the first author, followed by the abbreviation *et al.* (for *and others* in Latin). You should match the style used in your list of works cited.

> One position is that "in cultures whose religion, unlike Christianity, offers no promise of an afterlife, a name that will live on after one's death serves as the closest substitute for immortality" (Abrams et al. 3).

Corporate Author

A corporate author is a company, agency, or institution that is credited with authorship of a work. The corporate name should be treated the same as the name of an individual author. Place the name either in the preceding text or within the parenthetical reference.

> The Toyota brochure states that "every Toyota built in Canada has a recyclable content of at least 85%—and meets or exceeds today's most stringent emission standards" (6).

Unknown Authors

If the author of a work is not known, use the entire title in the preceding text or a short version of the title in the parenthetical reference.

> German authorities had drafted legislation to "ban the sale and importation of 'dangerous dogs,' but not limited to pit bulls, Staffordshire bull terriers and American Staffordshire terriers" ("Breed Ban" 8).

Multivolume Work

If you cite specific material from a multivolume work, include in the parenthetical reference the volume number, followed by a colon, a space, and then the page reference. Do not include *vol.* or *volume*, just the volume number.

> Abrams et al. state that "the period of more than four hundred years that followed the Norman Conquest presents a much more diversified picture than the Old English period" (1: 5).

If you are referring to an entire volume of a multivolume work, however, no page numbers will be cited; in this situation, put a comma after the author name and include the abbreviation of *volume*: (Abrams et al., vol. 1).

Fiction, Poetry, and Drama

Literary works are often available in different editions, so you must include information that will help readers to locate a reference in their particular editions, using abbreviations such as *ch.*, *pt.*, or *sec.*

Novel: When citing a passage from a novel (particularly one that may appear in several different editions) in the parenthetical reference, first provide the page reference and then, after a semicolon, give the part or chapter number where the passage can be found.

> In Atwood's The Robber Bride, Tony reveals a distorted picture of Zenia: "She has thought of Zenia as tearless, more tearless even than herself. And now there are not only tears but many tears, rolling fluently down Zenia's strangely immobile face, which always looks made-up even when it isn't" (190; ch. 25).

Poetry: When citing lines from poems, first give a part or subdivision reference, if one exists; then, give the line numbers. Use a period with no space after it between the two parenthetical pieces of information.

> In "Civil Elegies," Lee describes Canadians' relationship with the rugged land:
>
> > We lie on occupied soil.
> > Across the barren Shield, immortal scrubland and our own,
> > where near the beginning the spasm of lava
> > settled to bedrock schist,
> > barbaric land, initial, our
> > own, scoured bare under
> > crush of glacial recessions (3.40–46)

Drama: For a play, include the act, scene, and line numbers in the parenthetical reference of your citation, using Arabic numerals.

> Shakespeare establishes the dark mood of Macbeth in the second witch's response to the first witch's query on when they should meet again: "When the battle's lost and won" (1.1.4).

Bible

When citing a passage from the Bible, include—in either the preceding text or the parenthetical reference—the title, the book of the Bible, the chapter, and the verse. Books of the Bible may be abbreviated in a parenthetical reference, if you wish.

> The language of Exodus takes on a poetic, rhythmical quality: "He made the holy anointing oil also, and the pure fragrant incense, blended as by the perfumer" (The Holy Bible, 37.29).

A Work from an Anthology

When citing a specific work from an anthology, provide the name of the author of the piece you are using in the preceding text or parenthetical reference. Do not use the name of the anthology's editor (unless you are citing the entire anthology); the work should appear under its author's name here and in the Works Cited list.

> In "Silent Snow, Secret Snow," Conrad Aiken provides a vivid, poetic description of the young protagonist's growing detachment: "The hiss was now becoming a roar—the whole world was a vast moving screen of snow—but even now it said peace, it said remoteness, it said cold, it said sleep" (187).

An Indirect Source

Use original sources wherever possible. Occasionally, however, you may need to use material from indirect sources. If you must cite an author quoted in a work by another writer, begin the citation in the parenthetical reference with the abbreviation *qtd. in* (for *quoted in*).

> To Woody Allen, the successful monologue is a matter of attitude: "I can only surmise that you have to give the material a fair shake at the time and you have to deliver it with confidence" (qtd. in Lax 134).

An Entire Work

To cite an entire book or article, provide the author's name in the preceding text or in a parenthetical reference. No page reference is required.

> In <u>The Second Sex</u>, Simone de Beauvoir brilliantly argues her position on women's inequality.
>
> De Beauvoir argues her position on women's inequality brilliantly (<u>Second Sex</u>).

Electronic Sources

The MLA guidelines governing in-text citations for electronic sources are the same as those governing print sources such as books and articles. The following are situations you may encounter when citing electronic sources:

- *The electronic source has an author and fixed page numbers:* When the electronic source has an author and fixed page numbers, provide both. However, do not cite the page numbers of a printout of a document on the Web, as these will vary from printout to printout. The author's name might appear in the preceding text or the parenthetical reference.

According to Caroline Spurgeon, "The main image in Othello is that of animals in action, preying upon one another, mischievous, lascivious, cruel or suffering, and throughout the general sense of pain and unpleasantness is much increased and kept constantly before us" (2).

- *The electronic source has an author but no page number:* If the electronic source uses some other means of numbering, such as by paragraphs or sections, specify them by using the abbreviations *par.* or *pars.*, *sec.*, or the full word *screen* (or *screens*).

Fackrell asserts the accommodation for animals is adequate: "We have lodgings for up to 12 dogs at a time in our indoor/outdoor runs" (par. 9).

- *The electronic source has no author:* If the author of the electronic source is not known, use either the complete title in the preceding text or a shortened form of the title in the parenthetical reference.

According to the Web page sponsored by Children Now, an American organization that provides support for children and families, "52% of girls and 53% of boys say there are enough good role models for girls in television, although more girls (44%) than boys (36%) say there are too few" ("Reflections in Media").

MLA LIST OF WORKS CITED

When using the MLA documentation style, compile a list of works cited at the end of your paper. The list provides essential publication information for each of the sources cited in your paper. Include in your list of works cited only the sources from which you quoted, paraphrased, or summarized information. Do not include sources that you consulted but did not refer to in your paper. (Some instructors may require an additional list of works consulted.) See page 122 for a model Works Cited list.

BOOKS IN MLA STYLE

STANDARD FORMAT FOR ONE AUTHOR

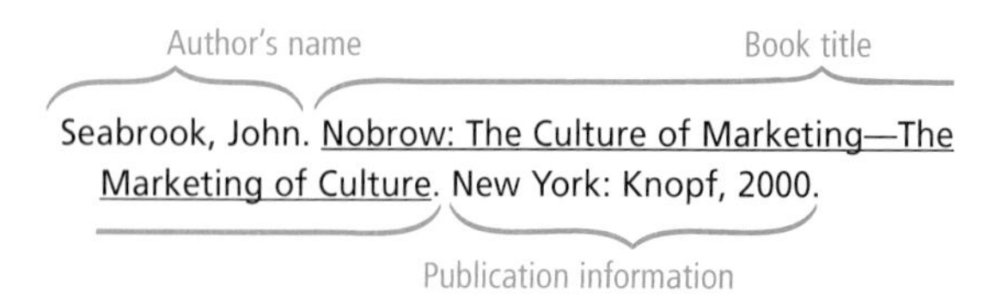

The information needed to write an entry for a book in your list of works cited is found on the **title page** at the front of the source and on the reverse side of the title page, which is known as the **copyright page**. A very few books have publication information at the back of the book. When writing an entry, use information from the source itself as opposed to information from a bibliography or library catalogue. This will reduce the chance of errors in your entry.

Author's name: Give the author's name exactly as it appears on the title page of the book. Place the author's last name first, followed by his or her first name and any initials that appear on the title page. Leave a space between each initial. Use a comma, followed by a space, to separate the author's first and last names. End the name segment with a period.

Book title: Provide the full name of the book, including any subtitles. The entire title should be underlined (or italicized, although MLA prefers underlining for student papers) except for the period that follows it. Capitalize important words within the title (see page 92). If there is a subtitle, separate the subtitle from the main title with a colon and one space. Always capitalize the first and last words in any subtitle. End the title with a period and leave one space before beginning the publication information.

For titles within underlined titles:

- If the title within a title would normally be underlined, neither underline it nor place it in quotation marks.

White, E. B. Writings from The New Yorker 1927–1976. Ed. Rebecca M. Dale. New York: HarperPerennial, 1991.

- Use quotation marks where you would normally do so.

Card, James Van Dyck. An Anatomy of "Penelope." Rutherford: Farleigh Dickinson UP, 1984.

For a title within a title in quotation marks:

- Underline if that is what you would normally do.
- If you would normally use quotation marks, use single quotation marks.

Publication information: Publication information includes the following:

- *Place of publication:* If several cities are listed on the title or copyright pages, record only the first city. Place a colon and one space between the place of publication and the name of the publisher. If, but only if, the place of publication is not well known or if its name is ambiguous, also give the province or state (use postal code abbreviations), or the country, in abbreviated form. (For example, if London, Ontario, is meant, rather than London, England, write *London, ON.*) Separate the city and the province, state, or country with a comma. For foreign-language works, if the name of the place of publication on the title page is not easily recognizable, you may put the English translation after it in square brackets.

- *Publisher*: You do not need to use the complete name of the publisher; simply give enough information to enable your reader to find the source easily. Omit any articles (*a*, *an*, *the*), common abbreviations such as *Inc.*, *Co.*, and *Ltd.*, and descriptive words, such as *Books*, *House*, *Press*, and *Publishers*. However, for university presses, always include the abbreviations *U* and *P*, or *UP*, as the case may be (e.g., *Oxford UP* or *U of Toronto P*. Some universities publish independently, so retaining the abbreviation avoids any confusion. If the publishing company is named after a person or persons, you may shorten it; for example, *W. W. Norton* should be reduced to *Norton*. Place a comma between the name of the publisher and the year of publication.
- *Year of publication*: If a number of years are listed on the title or copyright pages, use only the most recent one. Place a period after it.

Two or More Authors

McKercher, Catherine, and Carman Cumming. The Canadian Reporter: News Writing and Reporting. Toronto: Harcourt, 1998.

Separate the names of three authors with commas.

Petty, Walter T., Dorothy C. Petty, and Marjorie F. Becking. Experiences in Language: Tools and Techniques for Language Arts Methods. Boston: Allyn and Bacon, 1973.

More Than Three Authors

Newman, Garfield, et al. Canada: A Nation Unfolding. Toronto: McGraw-Hill Ryerson, 2000.

Editor(s)

Richler, Mordecai, ed. The Best of Modern Humour. Toronto: McClelland & Stewart, 1983.

Author with an Editor

Bronte, Charlotte. Jane Eyre. Ed. Susan Cockcroft. Cambridge, UK: Cambridge UP, 1996.

Translation

Apuleius. The Golden Ass. Trans. Jack Lindsay. Bloomington: Indiana UP, 1962.

Corporate Author

PriceWaterhouseCoopers Inc. Technology Forecast: 2000. Menlo Park, CA: PriceWaterhouseCoopers Technology Center, 2000.

Unknown Author

If the author of the source is unknown, begin the entry with the title of the work. In the Works Cited list, alphabetize the work by the first main word in the title. Do not consider initial articles (*A*, *An*, or *The*) when you alphabetize. In the example below, *Second* would be the word used to alphabetize.

"The Second Shepherds' Pageant." Everyman and Medieval Miracle Plays. Ed. A. C. Cawley. New York: Dutton, 1959.

Two or More Works by the Same Author

When you cite two or more works by the same author, provide the name of the author in the first entry only. In succeeding entries, type three hyphens followed by a period in place of the author's name.

Roth, Philip. The Human Stain. Boston: Houghton, 2000.

---. Patrimony: A True Story. New York: Simon, 1991.

However, if the second entry is a work co-authored by the author of (or leading author in) the first entry, do not use three hyphens; begin the second entry with the author's full name.

Edition Other Than the First

Strunk, William, Jr., and E. B. White. The Elements of Style. 3rd ed. New York: Macmillan, 1979.

Work in More Than One Volume

Place the number of volumes after the title and before the city of publication, using the abbreviation *vols.* (for *volumes*). If an editor or edition is listed after the title, place the number of volumes after that. Do not indicate any specific volume or page number(s) here; rather, supply these in the text.

Daymond, Douglas, and Leslie Monkman, eds. Literature in Canada. 2 vols. Toronto: Gage, 1978.

However, if you used only one of the volumes, indicate before the city name the volume you used by writing *Vol.* and the volume number. Give publication information for that volume only. Then, only page numbers are needed when you refer to this work in your text. You may, if you wish, indicate the total number of volumes at the end of the entry.

Daymond, Douglas, and Leslie Monkman, eds. Literature in Canada. Vol. 2. Toronto: Gage, 1978. 2 vols.

Encyclopedia, Dictionary, or Other Reference Work

Articles from well-known reference materials, such as standard dictionaries and encyclopedias, may be listed in a shortened form. List the following:

1. author of the article (if known)
2. title of the article, in quotation marks
3. title of the source
4. edition number (if there is one)
5. date of publication of the edition

Boles, Glen. "Mount Assiniboine." The Canadian Encyclopedia. 2000 ed. 1999.

The Bible

The Holy Bible: New Revised Standard Version. New York: Oxford UP, 1989.

Work in an Anthology

Fitzgerald, Penelope. "At Hiruharama." New Writing. Ed. Malcolm Bradbury and Judy Cooke. London, England: Minerva, 1992. 33–39.

Two or More Works from the Same Anthology

If you cite more than one work from an anthology, you may cross-reference. First provide a separate entry for the anthology with complete publication information.

Remnick, David, and Henry Finder, eds. Fierce Pajamas: An Anthology of Humor Writing from The New Yorker. New York: Random, 2001.

Next, list separately each anthology selection you wish to cite. For each, give the author and title of the selection, and cross-reference to the anthology by giving the last name(s) of the anthology editor(s). Provide the anthology page numbers where the selection appears.

Brickman, Marshall. "The Analytic Napkin." Remnick and Finder 25–28.

Geng, Veronica. "My Mao." Remnick and Finder 95–99.

Preface, Foreword, Introduction, or Afterword

Green, Richard. Introduction. The Consolation of Philosophy. By Boethius. Trans. Richard Green. Indianapolis: Bobbs-Merrill, 1962. ix–xxiii.

Book in a Series

Following the title of the work, give the series name (abbreviating words) with no underlining and the work's number within the series, if this information is available.

Lecker, Robert, Jack David, and Ellen Quigley. Bissoondath, Clarke, Kogawa, Mistry, Skvorecky. Can. Writers and Their Works 11. Toronto: ECW Press, 1996.

Republished Book

If the book is republished, place the original publication date after the title, then present new publishing information. When the republication includes new material, such as an afterword, include the information after the original publication date.

Moodie, Susanna. Roughing It in the Bush. 1852. Afterword Susan Glickman. Toronto: McClelland & Stewart, 1989.

ARTICLES IN PERIODICALS—MLA STYLE

Article in a Monthly Magazine

According to MLA style, periods follow the name of the author and the article title (in quotation marks, with the period inside). Next are the name of the magazine followed directly by the month or months and year and then a colon and space. With the exception of May, June, and July, abbreviate the months. For magazines, volume and issue number should not be included. Finally, the page numbers of the article are given, and a period ends the entry.

Bass, George F. "Golden Age Treasures." National Geographic Mar. 2002: 102–17.

If the article is printed on consecutive pages, give the inclusive page numbers. If not, give the first page number and a plus sign (+) to indicate that the page numbering is not continuous.

Article in a Weekly Magazine

Entries for a weekly magazine follow the same general pattern as those for a monthly magazine. However, provide the exact date of the issue, including the day, month, and year.

> Begley, Sharon. "The Schizophrenic Mind." Newsweek 11 Mar. 2002: 44–51.

Article in a Journal Paginated by Volume

> Strain, Laurel A. "Seniors' Centres: Who Cares?" Canadian Journal of Aging 20 (2001): 471–91.

Article in a Journal Paginated by Issue

> Frickle, Michele. "In This Pure Land." Surface Design Journal 25.3 (2002): 26–29.

Signed Article in a Daily Newspaper

> Conlogue, Ray. "All the News of 1752." Globe and Mail 4 Mar. 2002: R1+.

Unsigned Article in a Newspaper or Magazine

> "Northern Rockies Whopper." Beautiful British Columbia Spring 1998: 46.

Unsigned Editorial in a Newspaper

> "Where Justice Stumbled." Editorial. Globe and Mail 4 Mar. 2001: A10.

Letter to the Editor

> Kennedy, Paul. Letter. Harper's Sept. 2002: 4.

Book Review

> Gartner, Zsuzsi. "In Search of a Vanished Zeitgeist." Rev. of The Doctor's House, by Ann Beattie. Globe and Mail 2 Mar. 2002: D3.

Film Review

> Ansen, David. "Brave Heart of Darkness." Rev. of We Were Soldiers, dir. Randall Wallace. Newsweek 11 Mar. 2002: 63.

ELECTRONIC SOURCES IN MLA STYLE

Citations for electronic sources serve the same purposes as do citations for print sources, and there are similarities in their formats. However, a reader requires additional information to locate many electronic sources.

Bear in mind that, for electronic sources, documentation styles are still evolving. Often, updates can be found online. MLA guidelines for online citations can be accessed through the Internet at the following URL (click on "MLA Style" and then on "Frequently Asked Questions"):

- http://www.mla.org

The Columbia Guide to Online Style, developed by Janice Walker, presents a documentation style for online sources that can be used in combination with other styles. You can access information about *The Columbia Guide to Online Style* at the following URL:

- http://www.columbia.edu/cu/cup/cgos/idx_basic.html

ONLINE SOURCES

The list below indicates the information to include in a Works Cited entry for an online source and the order in which to present it. No single source will require all the items on the list. After the list, examples are given for various types of electronic sources.

Often, when you cite an online research source, the problem won't be deciding how much to include, but rather a shortage of available information. Include as many as you can of the following, if available and applicable:

1. *Author, etc.*: Name of the author of the source, last name first. (If the main creator of a source is an editor, compiler, or translator, give this name instead, followed by the appropriate abbreviation; for example, ed.)
2. *"Title A"*: Title of a poem, short story, article, or similar short work within a scholarly project, database, or periodical; or title of a posting to a discussion list or forum (take this from the subject line; after its end period write *Online posting* and a period). All these titles should be placed in quotation marks.
3. <u>Title B</u>: Title of a book, underlined or italicized.
4. *Editor, etc.*: Name(s) of the editor(s), compiler, or translator of the text (unless this information has already been given in the "author" section). Before the name include *Ed.*, *Comp.*, or *Trans.*, as appropriate.

5. *Print publication information:* Publication details about any print version of the source, including date of original print publication.
6. Title C: Title of the Internet site (e.g., scholarly project or database; periodical; or website, professional or personal). If there is no title, give the title as *Home page*, not underlined.
7. *Internet site editor:* Name(s) of the editor(s) or director of the scholarly project, database, periodical, or professional or personal website. Before the name(s) include *Ed.*, *Eds.*, or *Dir.*, as appropriate.
8. *Version:* Version number of the source (if not part of the title); for example, *Vers. 2.0*; or the volume and issue number for a periodical (not underlined, and with no punctuation between these elements and the name of the periodical).
9. *Date 1:* Date of electronic publication, of the latest update, or of posting. For a scholarly journal, the year of publication is enclosed in parentheses following the volume and issue information.
10. *Service:* Name of the subscription service by which the work was supplied (if applicable). If a library is the subscriber, include the library name and city (and province or state abbreviation, if needed), separated by commas.
11. *List or forum:* For a posting to a discussion list or forum, the name of the list or forum.
12. *Pages:* The number range (for example, 16–27) or total number of pages (*pp.*), paragraphs (*pars.*), or other sections (*secs.*), if they are numbered; for periodicals, this information follows a colon and space, as usual.
13. *Sponsor:* Name of any institution or organization sponsoring or associated with the website.
14. *Date 2:* Date you accessed the source.
15. *URL:* Complete electronic address, or URL, of the source (in angle brackets) or, for a subscription service, the URL of the service's main page (if known) or the keyword assigned by the service. Include the access-mode identifier (*http*, *ftp*, *gopher*, *telnet*, *news*) and any relevant path and file names. If a URL runs over a line, break it only after a slash and make sure no hyphens are inadvertently added at line breaks. A final period appears after the closing angle bracket containing the URL.

End the information that relates to each numbered item with a period, except after the title of a periodical and after the date you accessed the source.

In general, follow the print guidelines for details on setting up any given portion of the entry, such as title or publication information.

Source in Scholarly Project or Reference Database

"Charles George Douglas Roberts." The Electronic Text Centre. Dir. Alan Burk. 1996. U of New Brunswick Libraries. 5 Mar. 2002 <http://www.lib.unb.ca/Texts/research.htm>.

Frost, Robert. "Mowing." A Boy's Will. New York: Henry Holt, 1915. Project Bartleby Archive. Ed. Steven van Leeuwen. Dec. 1995. Columbia U. 6 Mar. 2002 <http://www.bartleby.com/117/19.html>.

Entire Online Scholarly Project

Early Modern English Dictionaries Database. Ed. Ian Lancashire. 1999. U of Toronto. 7 Mar. 2002 <http://www.chass.utoronto.ca/english/ emed/emedd.html>.

Professional or Personal Website

Lancashire, Ian. Home page. 28 Jan. 2002. 8 Mar. 2002 <http://www.chass.utoronto.ca/~ian/>.

Epic Records. 2001. Sony Music Inc. 18 Mar. 2002 <http://www.epicrecords.com>.

Online Book

Austen, Jane. Pride and Prejudice. 1813. Ed. Henry Churchyard. 1996. 12 Apr. 2002 <http://www.pemberley.com/janeinfo/pridprej.html>.

Online Book in Scholarly Project or Reference Database

Dickens, Charles. A Tale of Two Cities. 1859. An Online Library of Literature. Ed. Peter Galbavy. 29 June 1999. 17 Mar. 2001 <http://www.literature.org/authors/dickens-charles/two-cities/>.

Article in Online Scholarly Journal

Herman, David. "Sciences of the Text." Postmodern Culture 11.3 (May 2001): 29 pars. 16 Mar. 2002 <http://www.iath.virginia.edu/pmc/text-only/issue.501/11.3herman.txt>.

Article in Online Magazine

Nyham, Brendan. "Spinsanity." Salon 5 Mar. 2002. 7 Mar. 2002 <http://www.salon.com/politics/col/spinsanity/2002/03/05/dissent/index.html>.

Article in Online Newspaper

Webber, Terry. "Bank of Canada Stand Pat." GLOBEANDMAIL.com 5 Mar. 2002. 6 Mar 2002 <http://www.globeandmail.com>.

E-Mail

When citing information you received through electronic mail, begin with the e-mail author's name and then include the subject line in quotation marks. Write *E-mail to* followed by *the author* or the name of the person who received the e-mail. Then give the date it was received.

Chamberlain, Tim. "Re: Credibility in Magazines." E-mail to the author. 12 Nov. 2001.

Single-Edition CD-ROMs

The Rosetta Stone. CD-ROM. Harrisburg, VA: Fairfield Language Technologies, 1995.

OTHER SOURCES IN MLA STYLE

Government Publications

If you do not know the author of the work, consider the government agency as the author. Give the name of the government followed by the name of the agency.

Ontario. Ontario Human Rights Commission. Human Rights: Employment Application Forms and Interview. Toronto: Ontario Human Rights Commission, 1991.

If the author is known, you may start with either the author's name or the name of the agency; if the latter, give the author's name after the title of the work, preceded by By.

Pamphlet

The citation for a pamphlet follows the same pattern as that for a book.

Canada Revenue Agency. You've Got Tax Questions? We've Got the Answers! Quickly and Easily! Ottawa: Canada Revenue Agency, 2004.

Published Dissertation

Haas, Arthur G. *Metternich, Reorganization and Nationality, 1813–1818.* Diss. U of Chicago, 1963. Knoxville: U of Tennessee P, 1964.

Unpublished Dissertation

Mercer, Todd. "Perspective, Point of View, and Perception: James Joyce and Fredric Jameson." Diss. U of Victoria, Victoria, BC, 1987.

Lecture or Public Address

To cite a lecture or public address, first give the speaker's name and then the title of the lecture or address in quotation marks. Next, provide the name of the organization sponsoring the lecture or address, then the location and the date it was given.

Hill, Larry. "Navigating the Void and Developing a Sense of Identity." Traill College, Trent University, Peterborough, ON. 30 Jan. 2002.

Interview

Smith, Michael. Interview. *Morningside.* CBC-AM Radio, Toronto. 10 Oct. 1993.

If you cite information from an interview you have conducted, record the name of the person interviewed, then write *Personal interview* or *Telephone interview* or some other such description, and then the date of the interview.

Henry, Martha. Personal Interview. 19 Apr. 1998.

Film, Videotape, or DVD

After the title, name the director, preceded by *Dir.* For a film, you may then name the writer, major actors, narrator, or producer, if relevant, indicating roles using the appropriate abbreviation(s), for example, *Perf.* for performers.

Othello. Dir. Stuart Burge. Perf. Laurence Olivier, Maggie Smith, Joyce Redman, and Frank Finlay. Warner Bros., 1965.

For a videotape or DVD, include *Videocassette* or *DVD* before the distributor's name.

The Big Snit. Dir. Richard Condie. Videocassette. National Film Board of Canada, 1985.

Radio or Television Program

"In on the Action." The Fifth Estate. CBC-TV. CBLT, Toronto. 6 Mar. 2002.

Live Performance

After the title, give the name(s) of the playwright or choreographer, director, performers, and so on, the name of the theatre or hall and its location, and the date of the performance.

Indian Ink. By Tom Stoppard. Dir. Richard Cottrell. Perf. Fiona Reid. Bluma Appel Theatre, Toronto. 1 Apr. 2002.

Sound Recording

The artist's name you list first depends on what aspect of the recording you wish to emphasize. Next list the title of the work (underlining album titles but putting single songs, etc., in quotation marks); other artists; and the manufacturer and year of issue.

Verdi, Guiseppe. Arias. Perf. Simon Estes. New Philharmonic Orchestra. Cond. Gaetano Delogu. Philips, 1987.

MLA INFORMATION NOTES

Two types of optional information notes may be used with the MLA parenthetical documentation style:

1. *Content notes:* Content notes should be brief and give the reader important additional information that would have interrupted the flow of ideas in the text.
2. *Bibliographic notes:* Bibliographic notes provide the reader commentary on sources and may be useful when referring to numerous sources or to additional reading not cited in the text itself.

Options for Information Notes

There are two appropriate locations for information notes in your research paper:

1. At the bottom of the page, where the information note appears as a footnote.
2. At the end of the research paper, just before the list of works cited. In this case the notes are called endnotes.

Setting up Information Notes

Indicate an information note by placing a raised (superscript) Arabic number at the appropriate place in the text and write the note with a corresponding numeral, either as a footnote at the bottom of the page or as an endnote in the endnotes list. Try to organize your text sentence so the need for an information note falls at the end of a sentence. Ideally, the number in the text signalling the note should appear after end-of-sentence punctuation.

Number information notes consecutively throughout the paper whether you are using the footnote or endnote system. Leave one space before the number, and raise the number slightly above the line of words, then leave one space after the note number before beginning the next sentence.

When starting an information note either at the bottom of the page or in your endnotes list, indent the first line five spaces and use a superscript Arabic number. After the note number, leave one space and begin the words of your information note. Do not indent any line after the first. Double-space each note and between notes.

Start endnotes on a separate page at the back of the research paper. From the top edge of the page drop down 1.25 cm and centre the title *Notes*.

The example below illustrates the relationship between the note number in the text and the information note at the bottom of the page or in the endnotes.

Placing the Information Note in the Text

Circumnavigation of any large land body in a kayak requires significant, time-consuming preparation.[1]

Writing the Information Note

[1] For a full discussion of the preparation required, see Fenger 32.

In this case, the bibliographic information note refers the reader to another source, which is described in detail in the list of works cited.

MLA MANUSCRIPT FORMAT

The formatting of the sample research paper—an actual student paper—presented in this section is consistent with the recommendations provided in the *MLA Handbook for Writers of Research Papers* (6th ed., 2003).

Another source you might consult for more detailed information about MLA format and documentation style is the *MLA Style Manual and Guide to Scholarly Publishing* (2nd ed., 1999).

SAMPLE PAPER: MLA STYLE

The following sample pages from an essay by university student Dan McKeown on cultural aspects of E. M. Forster's novel *A Passage to India* illustrate some important features of MLA style.

McKeown 1

Dan McKeown

Dr. S. O. O'Brien

English 4W03

26 November 2005

Title is centred and double-spaced.

"The White Man's Burden" and Characterization in

E. M. Forster's A Passage to India

The most fundamental way to describe "the white man's burden," especially in a historical-literary context, is to understand it as an extension of Edward Said's principle of Orientalism. As Said explains, Orientalism is a way of organizing and understanding "truths" about the East. The British, for example, establish and understand a system of knowledge about India by opposing the racial "truths" of "us" and "them" (Said 1279–80).

Citation includes author's name and page number in parentheses.

Author is named in preceding text, so only page number is given in parentheses at end of paraphrase.

When the British physically enter India, however, this knowledge must somehow be transferred from the British imagination and, in a sense, "re-projected" onto India so that it can be actualized in the operation of the Empire. As Said explains, the Westerner creates "a whole series of possible relationships with the Orient" without ever relinquishing his or her hegemony (1281). "The white man's burden" was one such relationship. Between the late nineteenth century and World War II, "the white man's burden" was the underlying ideology of Britain's Imperial relationship with India. Straightforward and relatively uniform in Britain, the "burden" was to "civilize" India. In India itself, however, the relationship was conflicted and certainly not uniform. As E. M. Forster demonstrates in A Passage to India, the main characters (British and Indian) of Chandrapore have highly conflicted views about the role of the white man in India. Ultimately, Forster uses his characters to demonstrate the impossibility of engaging Orientalist "truths" about Indians via "the white man's burden."

Thesis states writer's conclusions about the novel.

List is alphabetized by the authors' last names.

List of works cited begins on a separate page.

Works Cited

Armstrong, Paul. "Reading India: E. M. Forster and the Politics of Interpretation." Twentieth-Century Literature: A Scholarly and Critical Journal 18.4 (1992): 365–85.

Forster, E. M. A Passage to India. London, England: Penguin, 1979.

Heath, Jeffrey. "A Voluntary Surrender: Imperialism and Imagination in A Passage to India." U of Toronto Quarterly 59 (1998–99): 287–309.

Kipling, Rudyard. "The White Man's Burden." The Writings in Prose and Verse of Rudyard Kipling. Vol. 21. New York: Scribner's, 1903. 36 vols.

Lawrence, James. "The White Man's Burden? Imperial Wars in the 1890s." History Today 42 (1992): 45–51.

Lin, Lidan. "The Irony of Colonial Humanism." Review of International English Literature 28 (1997): 133–53.

Loeb, Kurt. White Man's Burden. Toronto: Lugus, 1992.

Meyers, Jeffrey. Fiction and the Colonial Experience. Totowa, NJ: Rowman & Littlefield, 1973.

Said, Edward. "From the Introduction to Orientalism." The Critical Tradition. Ed. David Richter. Boston: Bedford, 1998. 1278–92.

Van Creveld, Martin. The Rise and Decline of the State. Cambridge, UK: Cambridge UP, 1999.

Each entry is a hanging indent, where the first line is typed flush left.

APA Style of Documentation

In APA in-text citation, you include the date of the publication, while in the MLA style you do not. Documentation guidelines outlined in this section are consistent with those provided in the *Publication Manual of the American Psychological Association*, 5th ed. (Washington: APA, 2001).

IN-TEXT CITATIONS: APA STYLE

APA in-text citations identify any research source used in a paper by the author's name and the year of publication. For direct quotations from a source, page numbers are provided as well. The in-text citations direct the reader to a list of references at the end of the paper, where information needed to locate the sources is provided.

STANDARD APA FORMAT FOR A QUOTATION

> Peter Newman (1995) observes, "As the institutional touchstones that had once been the nation's Pole Star fell away, Canadians began automatically to distrust anyone who exercised authority over their lives" (p. 183).

If the author's name is not provided in the preceding text, give the author's last name, the date of publication, and the page reference in parentheses after the direct quotation. Use commas to separate units of information within the parenthetical reference.

> One observer notes, "As the institutional touchstones that had once been the nation's Pole Star fell away, Canadians began automatically to distrust anyone who exercised authority over their lives" (Newman, 1995, p. 183).

STANDARD APA FORMAT FOR A SUMMARY OR PARAPHRASE

You can provide the author's name and the date of publication either in the preceding text or as a parenthetical reference after a summary or paraphrase. Page numbers are not required, but their use is suggested when citing longer works, to help readers locate specific information.

> According to Newman (1995), Canadian banking was highly conservative prior to the mid-1980s, and a particular bank stayed with a company for a long period of time.

> In the conservative era of Canadian banking, one commentator observes that the only way for a bank to be dismissed was if embezzlement was taking place or employees were organizing a tellers' union (Newman, 1995).

Two Authors

For a work with two authors, always give both authors' names and the year of publication with every reference in the text, or put both names and the publication date in a parenthetical reference at the end of the relevant sentence. In the parenthetical reference, use the ampersand (&) instead of *and*.

> Clarkson and McCall (1990) agree that Trudeau's writings during the early 1960s revealed him at the height of his powers as a writer and Quebec theoretician on federalism.

> During the early 1960s, Trudeau was at the height of his powers as a writer and was viewed as the preeminent Quebec theoretician on federalism (Clarkson & McCall, 1990).

Three to Five Authors

First Citation of the Source

> Effective class groups do not happen randomly; however, an instructor can encourage their development by employing effective teaching methods and monitoring group performance (Lang, McBeath, & Hebert, 1995).

Subsequent Citation of the Source

> Classroom management approaches can be classified by the degree of teacher intervention and the control that each approach needs (Lang et al., 1995).

Six or More Authors

> Many assert that Canada's involvement in World War I was characterized by racism in some instances and by greed and corruption in others (Newman et al., 2000).

Author Unknown

When the author is unknown, use the title of the work in the text or provide a shortened version of the title in the parenthetical reference.

> According to the editorial "TTC the Big Loser in Shoestring Budget" (2002), the problems facing Canada's largest subway system can be remedied only through federal funding.

> The problems facing Canada's largest subway system can be remedied only through federal funding ("TTC Big Loser," 2002).

Corporate Author

Entry in Reference List: Assembly of First Nations. (2000).
First Citation: (Assembly of First Nations [AFN], 2000)
Subsequent Citations: (AFN, 2000)

Personal Communications

Communications such as letters, memos, and e-mails should be acknowledged by giving the initial and last name of the person with whom you communicated and the date on which the communication took place. You do not need to include these items in your list of references.

> J. Nadler (personal communication, November 12, 1998) indicated that the Russian mafia played a significant role in supplying protection for Budapest nightclub owners.

Electronic Source

Follow the guidelines for print sources. However, many electronic sources do not provide page numbers. When paragraph numbers are given, use these in place of page numbers. Use the ¶ symbol or the abbreviation *para.*

> As Myers (2000, ¶ 7) aptly phrased it, "positive emotions are both an end—better to live fulfilled, with joy [and other positive emotions]—and a means to a more caring and healthy society."

APA REFERENCES

A sample APA References list is on page 133.

BOOKS IN APA STYLE

Standard Book Format for One Author

McConnell, J. (1974). *Understanding human behavior: An introduction to psychology.* New York: Holt, Rinehart.

Two or More Authors

Krebs, D., & Blackman, R. (1988). *Psychology: A first encounter.* San Diego: Harcourt.

Griffin, R. W., Ebert, R. J., & Starke, F. A. (1999). *Business* (3rd Canadian ed.). Scarborough, ON: Prentice Hall.

Editor(s)

Fraser, K. (Ed.). (1991). *Bad trips.* Toronto: Random.

Translation

Barthes, R. (1987). *Mythologies* (A. Lavers, Trans.). London, England: Paladin Grafton Books. (Original work published 1957)

Note: In the text, cite both the original publication date and the date of translation, for example, (Barthes, 1957/1987).

Corporate Author

If the author of the source is a corporation, agency, or organization, the publisher is often the same as the organization. In such instances, use *Author* to indicate the publisher's name.

Ministry of Education and Training. (1990). *Ministry of Education and Training style guide for editors and writers.* Toronto: Author.

Unknown Author

German for travellers. (1986). Lausanne, Switzerland: Editions Berlitz.

Edition Other Than the First

Gifford, D. (1982). *Joyce annotated* (2nd ed.). Berkeley: University of California Press.

Article in an Edited Book

Bruce, H. (1988). Portugal. In K. Dobbs (Ed.), *Away from home: Canadian writers in exotic places* (pp. 297–301). Toronto: Deneau.

Multivolume Work

Mansion, J. E. (1974). *Harrap's new standard French and English dictionary* (Vols. 1–2). London, England: Harrap.

ARTICLES IN PERIODICALS APA STYLE

Article in a Journal Paginated by Volume

Dodd, D. (2001). Helen MacMurchy, MD: Gender and professional conflict in the medical inspection of Toronto schools, 1910–1911. *Ontario History, 93,* 127–149.

Article in a Journal Paginated by Issue

Martin, R. (2002). The virtue matrix: Calculating the return on corporate responsibility. *Harvard Business Review, 80*(3), 69–75.

Article in a Magazine

Tarry, C. (2002, March). The Danube: Europe's river of harmony and discord. *National Geographic, 201,* 62–79.

Article in a Newspaper

MacGregor, K. (2002, March 12). Zimbabwe voting ends in confusion. *The Globe and Mail*, p. A14.

Letter to the Editor

Marajh, T. (2002, March 12). Father was following natural love [Letter to the editor]. *Toronto Star*, p. A27.

Review

Chodoff, P. (2002). Redeeming Frieda [Review of the book *To redeem one person is to redeem the world: The life of Frieda Fromm-Reichmann*]. *Psychology Today, 35,* 76.

ELECTRONIC SOURCES IN APA STYLE

Updated information about documenting electronic sources and information from the latest APA publication manual can be found on the APA website at

- http://www.apastyle.org/elecref.html

Article Based on a Print Source

Many articles retrieved from online publications are duplicates of print versions; in these cases, follow the format of the print form. However, if you viewed the article only in electronic form, add [*Electronic version*] after the article title and before the name of the periodical.

Strain, L. A. (2000). Seniors' centres: Who cares? [Electronic version]. *Canadian Journal of Aging, 20,* 471–491.

Article in Online Journal

If the online article and the print article differ (e.g., page numbers are not included or additional information is given, or if you retrieved the article from an Internet-only journal), add the date you retrieved the document and the URL. Ideally, the URL should link directly to the article.

Sands, P. (2003, Fall). Pushing and pulling toward the middle. Kairos, 7(3). Retrieved May 2, 2003, from http://english.ttu.edu/kairos/7.3/binder2.html?coverweb.html#gender

An online periodical will not have page numbers and will often not use volume and issue numbers. If this is the case, simply provide the name of the periodical and the retrieval date and URL.

Smith, J. (2003, January 16). Journalism fails its sobriety test. Salon. Retrieved January 19, 2003, from http://www.salon.com/news/feature/2003/01/16/dui/index_np.html

Stand-Alone Document, No Author Identified, No Date

If the author of a document is not identified, begin the reference with the title of the document.

Erikson's development survey. (n.d.). Retrieved May 10, 2003, from http://www.hcc.hawaii.edu/intranet/committees/FacDevCom/guidebk/teachtip/erikson

Online Newsgroups, Forums, or Mailing Lists

To reference messages posted to archived online newsgroups, forums, or mailing lists, cite the author's name and the exact date of online posting. Follow this with the subject line of the posting and the address of the message group or forum, beginning with *Message posted to.*

Nivalainen, M. (2002, December 17). The key and stupid web moments of 2002 [Msg 3]. Message posted to Cybermind@listserv.aol.com

Article Retrieved from Database

McQueen, K. (2001, July 30). Bridges to our past. *Maclean's,* 114. Retrieved March 18, 2002, from Electronic Library database.

When obtaining material from a searchable, aggregated database, follow the appropriate format for the type of source retrieved and add a retrieval statement that gives the retrieval date and the name of the database. Many databases are available only through a centralized server (e.g., a university server); however, if the database is available only through an external website, the retrieval statement should include the appropriate URL.

Document on University Program or Department Website

Ludlow, P. (Ed.). (1996). *High noon on the electronic frontier: Conceptual issues in cyberspace.* Retrieved May 1, 2003, from Georgetown University, Communication, Culture and Technology Website: http://semlab2.sbs.sunysb.edu/Users/pludlow/highnoon

E-Mail

Do not include e-mails in the list of references, because e-mails are a form of personal communication. Cite them in the text only: (*Nelson Rafferty, personal communication, March 4, 2003*).

OTHER SOURCES IN APA STYLE

Dissertation Abstract

Karim, Y. (1999). Arab political dispute mediations (Doctoral dissertation, Wayne State University, 1999). *Dissertation Abstracts International*, 61, 350.

Government Document

Solicitor General of Canada. (1995). *Annual report on the use of electronic surveillance*. Ottawa: Author.

Conference Proceedings Published in a Book

Chorney, H. (1991). A regional approach to monetary and fiscal policy. In J. N. McCrorie & M. L. MacDonald (Eds.), *The constitutional future of the prairie and Atlantic regions of Canada* (pp. 107–121). Canadian Plains Research Center, University of Regina.

Note that regularly published conference proceedings are treated as periodicals.

Film, Videotape, or DVD

Alland, W. (Producer), & Arnold, J. (Director). (1954). *Creature from the black lagoon* [Motion picture]. United States: Universal Studios.

APA MANUSCRIPT FORMAT

The major formatting distinction between an MLA-style paper and an APA-style paper is that the APA paper has a separate title page. It may also have an abstract following the title page, and it is much more likely to include headings.

SAMPLE PAPER: APA STYLE

The sample pages on pages 131–33 are from a research paper written by university student Erika Smith as one of her humanities course requirements. As shown in these sample pages, Smith used the APA guidelines for manuscript formatting, including those for the title page, in-text citations, and documentation of sources. Smith's instructor required that students provide a title page with their papers but not an abstract, since the paper was to be fairly short.

Privacy Protection 1

Running head: PRIVACY PROTECTION ON THE INTERNET

Running head

Abbreviated title appears five spaces to the left of the page number, which is flush against the right margin. The paper's page numbering commences on the title page.

The full title is typed in upper- and lowercase, double-spaced, and centred just above the author's name.

The writer's name is centred approximately in the middle of the page.

Privacy Protection on the Internet:

An Evaluation of Policies and Regulations

Erika Smith

Humanities 1A03, Section 3

Professor Rockwell

March 25, 2005

Below the author's name is the course name and section number, the instructor's name, and the date the research paper was submitted.

Include full title, centred, at the beginning of the essay.

Privacy Protection on the Internet:

An Evaluation of Policies and Regulations

Because the authors' names do not appear in the preceding text, include them, with the date and page number, in parentheses. For the first citation of a work with three to five authors, cite all authors.

The Internet reaches nearly 50 million people worldwide, and this figure is growing at a rate of approximately 10% per month (Wang, Lee, & Wang, 1998, p. 63). It is a powerful medium, but its triumph as a global source of information will decline if proper privacy regulations are not enforced. At present, the issue of privacy protection remains unsolved. According to the Internet Society (2002), this is a problem that some legislators and companies are not interested in addressing:

Indent block quotations five spaces (about 1.25 cm).

> The universal acceptance of the technology that includes e-mail and the World Wide Web has made this technology an appealing tool for many who believe it is a justification for a change in the rules and expectations of privacy. The CEO of Sun Microsystems was widely quoted as saying "You have zero privacy anyway. Get over it." (Internet Society, 2002, ¶ 3)

Committees such as the World Wide Web Consortium (W3C) and the Platform for Privacy Preferences (P3) are trying to enjoin the government, private industry, and the user to resolve Internet problems. Three groups must work equally toward creating privacy: governments must cooperatively create universal legislation to regulate the Internet; the computer industry must have self-regulation policies; and Internet users must arm themselves against the invasion of privacy and contribute to the creation of legislation against the invasion of privacy.

Set up organization in the introduction.

References begin on a new page with this heading.

References

Engler, C. E. (1997, August). Trading in on some loss of personal privacy. *IEEE Spectrum*, *34*, 81–82.

Internet Society. (2002). *Internet privacy*. Retrieved March 3, 2003, from http://www.isoc.org/ internet/issues/privacy/

Kalin, S. (1997, January 3). *More grumbling about encryption export reform*. IDG News Service Online. Retrieved March 3, 2003, from http://www.pcworld.com/noews/daily/data/0197/97010311290.html

Madsen, W. (1998, June). Internet malcontents of the world--Unite! *Communications of the ACM*, *41*, 27–28.

Microsoft Corporation. (2001). *Safe internet: Microsoft privacy & security fundamentals*. Retrieved March 4, 2003, from http://www .microsoft.com/Privacy/SafeInternet/topics/browsing.htm

Wang, H., Lee, M. K. O., & Wang, C. (1998, March). Consumer privacy concerns about Internet marketing. *Communications of the ACM*, *41*, 63–70.

References are listed alphabetically by author's last name, and entries are double-spaced. In each entry, the second and subsequent lines are indented.

Chicago Style of Documentation

Documentation guidelines in this section are consistent with those provided in *The Chicago Manual of Style*, 15th ed. (Chicago: University of Chicago Press, 2003).

CHICAGO FOOTNOTES OR ENDNOTES

Guidelines for the *Chicago*-style documentation system follow. When using this system, provide complete bibliographic information when you cite a source for the first time. You must make a note to acknowledge any source you quote, paraphrase, or summarize. These notes can appear either together at the end of your research paper as **endnotes**, or at the foot of the page on which the citation appears as **footnotes**. *The Chicago Manual of Style* recommends the use of endnotes rather than footnotes if there are many notes or if the notes are long. To signal a note in the text, place a raised (superscript) Arabic numeral near the quoted, paraphrased, or summarized material (preferably at the end of the sentence, after any punctuation marks) to indicate that the information was obtained from another source. Number the notes consecutively throughout the paper. Readers can then find specific source information by locating the footnote or endnote with the corresponding number.

Sample Text Citation

"The possibility of a Marxist literary theory," in the words of Frow, "is given in the promise and the ambiguity of the central Marxist metaphors relating the symbolic order to the social process."[1]

As an endnote, or as a footnote at the bottom of the page, complete source information must appear in the format shown below. Always end a note with a period.

1. John Frow, Marxism and Literary History (Cambridge, MA: Harvard University Press, 1986), 7.

Subsequent Reference to the Source

Once you cite a source for the first time and fully document it, any subsequent reference to the source can be shortened. For most notes, this will mean giving the author's last name, followed by a comma and then the page number. If the work has no known author, a shortened version of the title can be used.

2. Frow, 156.

Multiple Works by the Same Author

If you need to acknowledge other works by the same author, give a short form of the title in subsequent citations. In general, do not shorten titles of five words or less, except to drop an initial article. Underline or italicize the title of a book; place the title of an article within quotation marks.

2. Frow, Marxism and Literary History, 156.

6. Frow, "Critical Mind," 10.

MODEL NOTES AND BIBLIOGRAPHIC ENTRIES

Entries in the following pages provide model notes and bibliographic entries for most of the types of resources you will use in your research.

BOOKS

Basic Format for a Book with One Author

1. Paul William Roberts, Empire of the Soul: Some Journeys in India (Toronto: Stoddart, 1994), 85–92.

Roberts, Paul William. Empire of the Soul: Some Journeys in India. Toronto: Stoddart, 1994.

Two or Three Authors

2. Ralph H. Johnson and J. Anthony Blair, Logical Self-Defence, 2nd ed. (Toronto: McGraw-Hill Ryerson, 1983), 17.

Johnson, Ralph H., and J. Anthony Blair. Logical Self-Defence, 2nd ed. Toronto: McGraw-Hill Ryerson, 1983.

Note that, in the bibliographic entry, the name of the first author is reversed (last name, then first) and that a comma precedes the *and* (or the next name, if there are three authors).

Unknown Author

3. The Millennium (Toronto: Globe and Mail in Education, 2000), 12.

The Millennium. Toronto: Globe and Mail in Education, 2000.

Edited Work without an Author

4. Pose Lamb and Richard Arnold, eds., Reading: Foundations and Instructional Strategies (Belmont, CA: Wadsworth, 1976), 29.

Lamb, Pose, and Richard Arnold, eds. Reading: Foundations and Instructional Strategies. Belmont, CA: Wadsworth, 1976.

Edited Work with an Author

5. John Stuart Mill, On Liberty, ed. Currin V. Shields (New York: Macmillan, 1956), 45–46.

Mill, John Stuart. On Liberty. Edited by Currin V. Shields. New York: Macmillan, 1956.

Translated Work

6. Jean-Paul Sartre, Iron in the Soul, trans. Gerard Hopkins (Harmondsworth, England: Penguin Books, 1978), 58.

Sartre, Jean-Paul. Iron in the Soul. Translated by Gerard Hopkins. Harmondsworth, England: Penguin Books, 1978.

Untitled Volume in a Multivolume Work

7. Magill's Medical Guide, vol. 1 (Pasadena, CA: Salem Press, 2002).

Magill's Medical Guide. Vol. 1. Pasadena, CA: Salem Press, 2002.

Note, however, that if specific pages in such a volume are cited, the note citation is set up differently (the bibliographic entry does not change).

8. Magill's Medical Guide (Pasadena, CA: Salem Press, 2002), 1: 63–67.

Titled Volume in a Multivolume Work

9. Stuart A. Kallen, ed., The 1400s, in vol. 5 of Headlines in History (San Diego, CA: Greenhaven Press, 2001), 50–55.

Kallen, Stuart A., ed. Headlines in History. Vol. 5, The 1400s. San Diego, CA: Greenhaven Press, 2001.

Work in an Anthology

10. Toni Morrison, "The Site of Memory," in Inventing the Truth: The Art and Craft of Memoir, ed. William Zinsser (Boston: Houghton Mifflin, 1998), 185–206.

Morrison, Toni. "The Site of Memory." In Inventing the Truth: The Art and Craft of Memoir, edited by William Zinsser. Boston: Houghton Mifflin, 1998.

Work in a Series

11. Robert Lecker, Jack David, and Ellen Quigley, Bissoondath, Clarke, Kogawa, Mistry, Skvorecky, Canadian Writers and Their Works, vol. 11 (Toronto: ECW Press), 1996.

Lecker, Robert, Jack David, and Ellen Quigley. Bissoondath, Clarke, Kogawa, Mistry, Skvorecky. Canadian Writers and Their Works, vol. 11. Toronto: ECW Press, 1996.

PERIODICALS

In the entries below, note that, while specific page references are given in the notes, inclusive pages for the article are given in the bibliographic entries.

Article in a Journal Paginated by Volume

12. Gregory J. Chaltin, "Computers, Paradoxes, and the Foundations of Mathematics," American Scientist 90 (2002): 165.

Chaltin, Gregory J. "Computers, Paradoxes, and the Foundations of Mathematics." American Scientist 90 (2002): 164–171.

Article in a Journal Paginated by Issue

13. Ann Beattie, "Real Place, Imagined Life," Literary Imagination: The Review of the Association of Literary Scholars and Critics 4, no. 1 (2002): 11.

Beattie, Ann. "Real Place, Imagined Life." Literary Imagination: The Review of the Association of Literary Scholars and Critics 4, no. 1 (2002): 10–16.

Article in a Magazine

14. Daniel Lazare, "False Testament: Archeology Refutes the Bible Claim to History," Harper's, March 2002, 40.

Lazare, Daniel. "False Testament: Archeology Refutes the Bible Claim to History." Harper's, March 2002, 39–47.

Article in a Newspaper

15. Randy Boswell, "Artists, Natives Renew Fight over Culture," Ottawa Citizen, March 12, 2002, A4.

In your bibliography, list only the newspaper itself and the inclusive dates of the issues you are citing in your paper.

Ottawa Citizen, March 4–April 3, 2002.

ELECTRONIC SOURCES

In general, *The Chicago Manual of Style* suggests that most electronic sources can be cited according to the guidelines for printed works, with the addition of a URL. The URL should take the reader directly to the source, and should be permanent enough to be available for the useful lifetime of the article or book that is cited.

Here is a model for Internet sources, illustrated in the examples that follow:

1. author's name, in normal order
2. document title, in quotation marks
3. title of complete work (if relevant), in italics or underlined
4. date of Internet publication or last revision
5. URL or other retrieval information
6. date of access, in parentheses
7. text division (if applicable)

WORLD WIDE WEB SITE

16. James Giblin, "Introduction: Diffusion and Other Problems in the History of African States," Art and Life in Africa Online, March 7, 1999, http://www.uiowa.edu/~africart/toc/history/giblistat.html (accessed March 15, 2002).

Giblin, James. "Introduction: Diffusion and Other Problems in the History of African States." Art and Life in Africa Online. March 7, 1999. http://www.uiowa.edu/~africart/toc/history/giblistat.html (accessed March 15, 2002).

E-MAIL MESSAGE

17. John Nadler, "Russian Mafia," personal e-mail, March 12, 2002.

Personal communications are rarely included in the bibliography.

ELECTRONIC DATABASE

18. James H. Wandergee, "Concept Mapping and the Cartography of Cognition," Journal of Research in Science Teaching 27, no. 4 (New York: Wiley, 1990), 925, Dialog, ERIC, EJ 463169. http://erie.ed.gov.

Wandergee, James H. "Concept Mapping and the Cartography of Cognition. Journal of Research in Science Teaching 27, no. 4. New York: Wiley, 1990. Dialog, ERIC, EJ 463 169. http://erie.ed.gov.

OTHER SOURCES

GOVERNMENT DOCUMENT

19. Health and Welfare Canada, A Vital Link: Health and the Environment in Canada (Ottawa: Minister of Supply and Services, 1992), 43.

Canada. Health and Welfare Canada. A Vital Link: Health and the Environment in Canada. Ottawa: Minister of Supply and Services, 1992.

SAMPLE PAGES: *CHICAGO* STYLE

The Chicago Manual of Style is designed primarily as a reference for professional writers and publishers rather than for students, and its guidelines are geared for work destined for publication. The sample pages provided on pages 140–42 will give you an idea of this style, however, based on the fifteenth edition of *The Chicago Manual of Style*. These sample pages illustrate how the student writer followed the *Chicago* guidelines for a page of text, a list of notes, and the bibliography.

CBE Style of Documentation

"CBE" stands for Council of Biology Editors, the former name of the Council of Science Editors (CSE). Full guidelines to the CBE style of documentation can be found in *Scientific Style and Format: The CBE Manual for Authors, Editors, and Publishers*, 6th ed. (New York: Cambridge University Press, 1994). While originally the *CBE Manual* focused on biology and medicine, the sixth, most recent edition covers all scientific disciplines.

The *CBE Manual* presents two styles of documentation.

1. In the **name–year** system, which is very similar to APA style and most often used in the biological and earth sciences, sources are identified in the text in parenthetical name–year references that lead to an alphabetical-by-author list of sources at the end of the manuscript. The most basic differences are that no comma follows the author's name in the parenthetical reference and no period is used after the abbreviation for pages (*p*).
2. The **citation-sequence** system, most often used in writing in the applied sciences, such as chemistry, computer science, mathematics, physics, and health, is outlined briefly below.

The page number appears in the upper right-hand corner. Numbering starts on the first page after the title page. Many instructors ask that you use your last name as a header.

Thorneloe 2

The Marxist critic Georg Lukacs, in rejecting modernist writers like James Joyce, suggests that their exaggerated concern for formal considerations--"experimental gimmicks" of style and literary technique--reflects a "tendency towards disintegration . . . [the] loss of artistic unity."[1] Fredric Jameson, a later Marxist critic, also observes fragmentation in literature of the Modernist period, which he identifies as exhibiting reifications. Jameson defines reification as

> a disease of that mapping function whereby the individual subject projects and models his or her own insertion into the collectivity. . . . The reification of late capitalism--the transformation of relations into an appearance of relationships between things--renders society opaque--it is the lived source of mystification on which ideology is based and by which domination and exploitation are legitimized.[2]

With the market exchange-value economy, people are commodified--they become depersonalized, reduced to mere things. We see evidence of this in Ulysses when Buck Mulligan remarks, "Redheaded women buck like goats," and when, through Father Conmee's intelligence, we learn "a tiny yawn opened the mouth of the wife of the gentleman with the glasses."[3] In both instances people are described in terms of things. Jameson suggests

The note number signals an acknowledgment. The number 2 corresponds to the second entry in the "Notes" section of the paper.

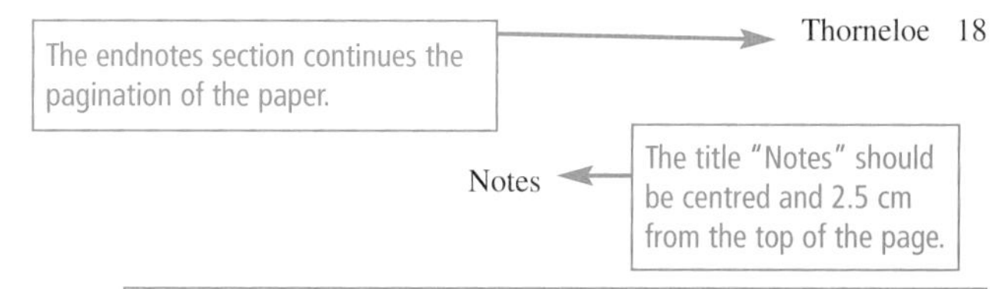

Indent the first line of the entry three or four spaces. Each subsequent line is flush with the left margin.

1. Georg Lukacs, Realism in Our Time (New York: Harper & Row, 1964), 37.

2. Fredric Jameson, "Reflections in Conclusion," Aesthetics and Politics, ed. Ronald Taylor (London, England: New Left Books, 1977), 212.

3. James Joyce, Ulysses (Harmondsworth, England: Penguin Books, 1985), 19, 183.

Numbers do not appear in superscript.

4. Georg Lukacs, The Meaning of Contemporary Realism (London, England: Merlin Press, 1979), 21.

5. Arthur Power, Conversations with James Joyce, ed. Clive Hart (Chicago: Univ. of Chicago Press, 1974), 95.

6. Richard Ellmann, James Joyce (Oxford, UK: Oxford Univ. Press, 1959), 459.

This note makes reference to a book that was cited earlier, so the entry can be shortened. The title is needed because the writer of the paper cited other works by the same author.

7. Lukacs, Meaning of Contemporary Realism, 39.

Authors' names appear with the first name first.

8. Hugh Kenner, Dublin's Joyce (Bloomington: Indiana Univ. Press, 1956), 60.

9. William C. Dowling, Jameson, Althusser, Marx: An Introduction to the Political Unconscious (Ithaca, NY: Cornell Univ. Press, 1984), 26.

10. Terry Eagleton, Marxism and Literary Criticism (London, England: Methuen, 1976), 27.

11. Marilyn French, "Joyce and Language," James Joyce Quarterly 19, no. 3 (1982): 240.

12. Raymond Williams, Marxism and Literature (Oxford, UK: Oxford Univ. Press, 1977), 39.

13. Gerard Gennette, Narrative Discourse: An Essay in Method (Ithaca, NY: Cornell Univ. Press, 1972), 246.

14. French, 249.

Single-space entries and double-space between entries.

The title "Bibliography" should be centred and 2.5 cm from the top of the page.

The bibliography continues the pagination of the paper.

Bibliography

The first line of an entry is flush with the left margin. Subsequent lines are indented three or four spaces.

Dowling, William C. Jameson, Althusser, Marx: An Introduction to the Political Unconscious. Ithaca, NY: Cornell Univ. Press, 1984.

Eagleton, Terry. Marxism and Literary Criticism. London, England: Methuen, 1976.

Ellmann, Richard. James Joyce. Oxford, UK: Oxford Univ. Press, 1959.

French, Marilyn. "Joyce and Language." James Joyce Quarterly 19, no. 3 (1982): 227–50.

Authors' names are reversed so the last name appears first. Entries are arranged in alphabetical order by the authors' last names.

Gennette, Gerard. Narrative Discourse: An Essay in Method. Ithaca, NY: Cornell Univ. Press, 1972.

Jameson, Fredric. "Reflections in Conclusion." Aesthetics and Politics. Edited by Ronald Taylor. London, England: New Left Books, 1977.

Joyce, James. Ulysses. Harmondsworth, England: Penguin Books, 1985.

Kenner, Hugh. Dublin's Joyce. Bloomington: Indiana Univ. Press, 1956.

Lukacs, Georg. The Meaning of Contemporary Realism. London, England: Merlin Press,

Single-space entries and double-space between entries.

---. Realism in Our Time. New York: Harper & Row, 1964.

Power, Arthur. Conversations with James Joyce. Edited by Clive Hart. Chicago: Univ. of Chicago Press, 1974.

Williams, Raymond. Marxism and Literature. Oxford, UK: Oxford Univ. Press, 1977.

When more than one work by an author is cited, you may use three hyphens in place of the author's name for entries after the first. Arrange such entries in alphabetical order by title, ignoring any initial articles (*A*, *An*, *The*).

IN-TEXT CITATIONS: CBE STYLE

In the CBE citation-sequence system, when you cite sources in your paper, mark them with numbers, starting with 1 and continuing throughout the paper. Preferably, you will use a superscript number, though you may also use a number in parentheses (1). If you repeat a source, use the same number that you assigned to it originally.

Place the number right after the reference in the text and before any punctuation[1]. If the sentence uses the authority's name, add the number after the name. If a single reference points to more than one source, list the source numbers in a series[1,4,7], separating numbers with a comma with no space after it and using a hyphen to show more than two inclusive source numbers[8-10].

> McCarthy and Masson[1] wrote a book that not only touched on a subject not much examined before—animals' emotions—but became a popular non-fiction work as well. It continues work that Charles Darwin had begun, and like Savage-Rumbaugh and Lewin's[2] work on Kanzi, the chimpanzee who understands a good deal of spoken English, it expands our notions of what constitutes animal intelligence.

When you list references at the end of the paper, list them according to the numbers used in your text and in numerical order. The references for the paragraph above would appear as follows:

> [1] McCarthy S, Masson JM. When elephants weep: the emotional lives of animals. New York: Delacorte; 1995. 291 p.
>
> [2] Savage-Rumbaugh ES, Lewin R. The ape at the brink of the human mind. New York: Wiley; 1994. 299 p.

CBE REFERENCES

GENERAL PAGE LAYOUT

Follow general student-paper conventions. Begin your reference list on a separate page with the centred title "References" or "Cited References" at the top. Single-space entries, leaving a space between them. Use the flush-left style for entries.

Book with One Author

> [1] Hawking SW. The universe in a nutshell. New York: Bantam; 2001. 216 p.

Book with More Than One Author

[2] McCarthy S, Masson JM. When elephants weep: the emotional lives of animals. New York: Delacorte; 1995. 291 p.

Edited Book

[3] Bowling AT, Ruvinsky A, editors. The genetics of the horse. New York: Oxford University Press; 2000. p 34–37.

Chapter from an Edited Book

[4] Polanyi JC. The transition state. In: Zewail AH, editor. The chemical bond: structure and dynamics. Boston: Academic Press; 1992. p 201–27.

Edition Other Than the First

[5] Lyon MF, Searle AG, editors. Genetic variants and strains of the laboratory mouse. 2nd ed. Oxford (UK): Oxford University Press; 1989. p 1–11.

Article in a Journal Paginated by Volume

[6] Reimann N, Barnitzeke S, Nolte I, Bullerdick J. Working with canine chromosomes: current recommendations for karyotype description. J Hered. 1999;90(1):31–34.

Article in a Journal Paginated by Issue

[7] Lee TG, Liu W, Polanyi JC. Photochemistry of advanced molecules. Surf Sci. 1999;426:173.

Article in a Journal with Discontinuous Pages

[8] Crews D, Gartska WR. The ecological physiology of the garter snake. Sci Am. 1981;245:158–64,166–8.

Electronic Sources in CBE Style

The approach to Internet sources given in the sixth edition of *Scientific Style and Format* is now outdated. The seventh edition will give new recommendations for citing electronic sources. In the meantime, CSE recommends that you visit the website of the National Library of Medicine, where a supplement provides detailed instructions for citing all types of material found on the Internet and includes many examples:

- http://www.nlm.nih.gov/pubs/formats/internet.pdf

GLOSSARY OF USAGE

GLOSSARY OF USAGE

The following glossary alphabetically lists some commonly confused words. Refer to it when you need a quick answer about proper word usage.

How Can the Glossary of Usage Help You?

The glossary will help you to make correct word choices in both your formal and informal writing and speaking. It will do this by providing the following information:

- definitions of words
- sample sentences using words correctly in context
- preferred formal usage for academic writing
- commonly confused words (*explicit, implicit*)
- non-standard vocabulary (*ain't*)
- colloquialisms (*flunk*)
- jargon (*finalize*)
- non-inclusive language (mankind)
- redundancies (*and ... etc.*)
- parts of speech for many words
- cross-references to other relevant *Checkmate* sections
- homophones (*night, knight*)
- common abbreviations
- prefixes (*dis-*) and suffixes (*-ness*)

a, an. Use *a* before a word that begins with a consonant sound, even if the word begins with a vowel. Use *an* before a word that begins with a vowel sound, even if the word begins with a consonant. Words beginning with the letter *h* often present problems. Generally, if the initial *h* sound is hard, use *a*. However, if the initial *h* is silent, use *an*. If the *h* is pronounced, Canadian writers generally use *a* with the word.

accept, except. *Accept* is a verb meaning "to receive" or "take to (oneself)." *Except* is very rarely a verb; usually, it is a preposition meaning "excluding."

adapt, adopt. *Adapt* means to "adjust oneself to" or "make suitable," and it is followed by the preposition *to*. The word *adapt* can also mean "revise," in which case it is used with the preposition *for* or *from*. *Adopt* means "to take or use as one's own."

adverse, averse. *Adverse* means "unfavourable." *Averse* means "opposed" or "having an active distaste"; or it means "reluctant," in which case it is followed by the preposition *to*.

advice, advise. *Advice* is a noun that means "an opinion about what should be done." *Advise* is a verb that means "to offer advice."

affect, effect. *Affect* is a verb that most commonly means "to influence." *Effect* is often a noun meaning "result." *Effect* can also be used as a verb meaning "to bring about or execute."

aggravate, irritate. *Aggravate* is a verb that means "to make worse or more severe." *Irritate*, a verb, means "to make impatient or angry." Note that *aggravate* is often used colloquially to mean *irritate*. Do not substitute *aggravate* for *irritate* in formal writing.

agree to, agree with. *Agree* to means "to consent to." *Agree with* mean "to be in accord with."

ain't. *Ain't* means "am not," "are not," or "is not." As it is non-standard English, it should not be used in formal writing.

all ready, already. *All ready* means "completely prepared." *Already* is an adverb that means "before this time; previously; even now."

all right, alright. *All right* is always written as two words. *Alright* is non-standard English for *all right* and should not be used in formal writing.

all together, altogether. See *altogether, all together.*

allude, elude. *Allude* means "to refer to indirectly or casually." Do not use it to mean "to refer to directly." *Elude* means "to evade or escape from, usually with some daring or skill," or "to escape the understanding or grasp of."

allusion, illusion, delusion. *Allusion* is an "implied or indirect reference." The word *illusion* means "an appearance or feeling that misleads because it is not real." This should be distinguished from *delusion*, which means "a false and often harmful belief about something that does not exist."

alot, a lot. A *lot* is always written as two words. Avoid using *a lot* in formal writing.

altogether, all together. *Altogether* means "completely, entirely." The phrase *all together* means "together in a group."

a.m., p.m., A.M., P.M. Use these abbreviations only with specific times, when numerals are provided: 10 *a.m.* or 1 *p.m.* Do not use the abbreviations as substitutes for *morning, afternoon,* or *evening*.

among, between. See *between, among*.

amoral, immoral. *Amoral* means "not having any morals; neither moral or immoral." The word *immoral* means "morally wrong or wicked."

amount, number. *Amount* is used to refer to things in bulk or mass. These things cannot be counted. *Number* is used to refer to things that can be counted.

an, a. See *a, an*.

and . . . etc. *Etc.* (*et cetera*) means "and so forth." Do not use and . . . *etc.* because it is redundant. See also *etc.*

and/or. *And/or* is sometimes used to indicate three possibilities: one, or the other, or both. It is occasionally acceptable in business, technical, or legal writing. Avoid this awkward construction when writing for the humanities.

ante-, anti-. *Ante-* is a prefix that means "before; earlier; in front of." The prefix *anti-* means "against" or "opposed to." Use *anti-* with a hyphen when it is followed by a capital letter (*anti-American*) or a word beginning with *i* (*anti-intellectual*). Otherwise, consult a dictionary.

anxious, eager. *Anxious* means "nervous," "troubled," or "worried." *Eager* means "looking forward" and is often followed by the preposition *to*. Do not use *anxious* to mean "eager."

anyone, any one. *Anyone* is an indefinite pronoun that means "any person at all." *Anyone* is singular. (See pages 10 and 22.) In *any one*, the pronoun *one* is preceded by the adjective *any*. Here the two words refer to any person or thing in a group.

anyplace. *Anyplace* is informal for *anywhere*. Do not use *anyplace* in formal writing.

anyways, anywheres. *Anyways* and *anywheres* are non-standard for *anyway* and *anywhere*, respectively. Always use *anyway* and *anywhere* in formal speaking and writing.

as. Substituting *as* for *because, since,* and *while* may make a sentence vague or ambiguous, making the cause–effect relationship unclear.

as, like. See *like, as*.

averse, adverse. See *adverse, averse*.

awful, awfully. In formal English usage the adjective *awful* means "filled with awe." Colloquially, *awful* is used to mean "bad" or "terrible." The adverb *awfully* is sometimes used in informal speech as an intensifier to mean "extremely" or "very." Avoid such colloquial usage in formal writing.

awhile, a while. *Awhile* is an adverb. Use the article and noun, *a while*, as the object of a preposition.

bad, badly. *Bad* is an adjective; *badly* is an adverb.

being as, being that. Both *being* as and *being that* are non-standard expressions used in place of the subordinate conjunctions *because* or *since*.

beside, besides. *Beside* is a preposition meaning "by the side of" or "near." *Besides* is a preposition meaning "also," "moreover," or "further." *Besides* can also be an adverb meaning "in addition."

between, among. Use *among* when referring to relationships involving more than two people or things. Use *between* when referring to relationships involving two people or things.

bring, take. Use *bring* when something is being moved toward the speaker. Use *take* when something is being moved away.

burst, bursted; bust, busted. *Burst* is an irregular verb meaning to "fly apart suddenly with force; explode; break open." *Bursted* is the non-standard past-tense form of *burst*. *Bust* and its past-tense form *busted* are slang.

can, may. *Can* means "know how to" or "be able to." *May* means "be allowed to" or "have permission to." The distinction in meaning between *can* and *may* is still made in formal writing. In informal English, *can* is widely used to mean both "be able to" and "be allowed to."

capital, capitol. *Capital* refers to a city where the government of a country, province, or state is located. *Capital* can also mean "the amount of money a company or person uses in carrying on a business." A *capitol* is a building in which American lawmakers meet. When referring to the building in which the U.S. Congress meets, capitalize the first letter, as in *Capitol*.

censor, censure. The verb *censor* means "to edit or remove from public view on moral or other grounds." The verb *censure* means "to express strong disapproval."

cite, site. The verb *cite* means "to quote, especially as an authority." The noun *site* often means "a particular place."

climactic, climatic. *Climactic* is an adjective derived from *climax*; *climax* means "the highest point; point of highest interest; the most exciting part." The adjective *climatic* means "of or having to do with climate."

coarse, course. *Coarse* usually means "heavy and rough in texture" or "crude." *Course* means "a line of movement," "a direction taken," "a way, path, or track," "a playing field," or "a series of lessons in a particular subject."

compare to, compare with. *Compare to* means "to represent as similar." *Compare with* means "to point out how two persons or things are alike and how they differ."

complement, compliment. The verb *complement* means "to reinforce, add to, or complete something." As a noun, *complement* is something that completes. *Compliment* as a verb means "to say something in praise." As a noun, *compliment* means "a remark of praise."

conscience, conscious. *Conscience* is a noun meaning "the sense of moral right and wrong." *Conscious* is an adjective that means "aware; knowing."

consensus of opinion. *Consensus* means "general agreement." As a result, the phrase *consensus of opinion* is redundant.

contact. *Contact* is often used informally as a verb meaning "to communicate with." In formal writing, use a precise verb such as *e-mail, telephone*, or *write*.

continual, continuous. *Continual* means "repeated many times; very frequent." *Continuous* means "without a stop or a break."

could care less. *Could care less* is non-standard and should not be used in formal writing. Use *couldn't care less* in its place.

could of. *Could of* is non-standard for *could have*.

council, counsel. *Council* is a noun used to describe "a group of people called together to talk things over, or give advice"; it also applies to "a group of people elected by citizens to make up laws." A *councillor* is a member of the *council*. *Counsel* as a noun means "advice," and as a verb, "to advise." *Counsel* can also mean a lawyer. A *counsellor* is someone who gives advice or guidance.

course, coarse. See *coarse, course*.

criteria, criterion. *Criteria* are rules for making judgments. *Criteria* is the plural form of *criterion*.

data, datum. *Data* are "facts or concepts presented in a form suitable for processing in order to draw conclusions." *Data* is the plural form of *datum*, which is rarely used. Increasingly *data* is used as a singular noun; however, careful writers use it as a plural.

delusion, illusion. See *allusion, illusion, delusion*.

differ from, differ with. *Differ from* means "to be unlike." *Differ with* means "to disagree with."

different from, different than. In standard English the preferred form is *different from*. However, *different than* is gaining wider acceptance, especially when *different from* creates an awkward construction.

discreet, discrete. *Discreet* means "prudent and tactful in speech and behaviour." *Discrete* means "separate; distinct."

disinterested, uninterested. *Disinterested* means "impartial." *Uninterested* means "lacking in interest," or "bored."

don't. *Don't* is a contraction for *do not*. Do not use *don't* as a contraction for *does not*; the correct contraction is *doesn't*.

due to. *Due to* means "caused by" or "owing to." It should be used as an adjective phrase following a form of the verb *to be*. In formal writing, *due to* should not be used as a preposition meaning "because of."

each. *Each* is singular. (See pages 10 and 22.)

eager, anxious. See *anxious, eager*.

effect, affect. See *affect, effect*.

e.g. This is the Latin abbreviation for *exempli gratia*, which means "for example." In formal writing, avoid *e.g.* and use phrases such as *for example* or *for instance* instead.

either. *Either* is singular. (See pages 10 and 22.) For *either . . . or* constructions, see pages 21–22.

elicit, illicit. *Elicit* is a verb meaning "to draw forth" or "bring out." The adjective *illicit* means "unlawful."

elude, allude. See *allude, elude*.

emigrate from, immigrate to. *Emigrate* means "to leave one's own country or region and settle in another"; it requires the preposition *from*. *Immigrate* means "to enter and permanently settle in another country"; it requires the preposition *to*.

eminent, immanent, imminent. *Eminent* means "distinguished" or "exalted." *Immanent* is an adjective that means "inherent" or "remaining within." *Imminent* is an adjective meaning "likely to happen soon."

enthused, enthusiastic. *Enthused* is an informal term meaning "showing enthusiasm." Use *enthusiastic* instead.

-ess. Many readers find the *-ess* suffix demeaning. Write *actor*, not *actress; singer*, not *songstress*.

etc. *Etc.* is an abbreviation that in English means "and other things." Do not use *etc.* to refer to people. In more formal writing, it is preferable to use the expression *and so on* in place of *etc.* See also *and . . . etc.*

eventually, ultimately. *Eventually* often means "an undefined time in the future." *Ultimately* commonly means "the greatest extreme or furthest extent." *Eventually* and *ultimately* are frequently used interchangeably. It is best to use *eventually* when referring to time and *ultimately* when referring to greatest extent.

everybody, everyone. *Everybody* and *everyone* are both singular. (See pages 10 and 22.)

everyone, every one. *Everyone* is an indefinite pronoun meaning "every person." *Every one* is a pronoun, *one*, modified by an adjective, *every*; the two words mean "each person or thing in a group." *Every one* is frequently followed by *of*.

except, accept. See *accept, except*.

except for the fact that. Avoid this wordy, awkward construction. Instead, use *except that*.

explicit, implicit. *Explicit* means "clearly expressed; directly stated." *Implicit* means "meant but not clearly expressed or directly stated."

farther, further. In formal English *farther* is used for physical distance. *Further* is used to mean "more" or "to a greater extent."

female, male. *Female* and *male* are considered jargon if substituted for "woman" and "man."

fewer, less. Use *fewer* only to refer to numbers and things that can be counted. Use *less* to refer to collective nouns or things that cannot be counted.

finalize. *Finalize* is a verb meaning "to bring to a conclusion." The word, though often used, is considered jargon by many people. Use a clear, acceptable alternative.

flunk. *Flunk* is colloquial for *fail*, and it should be avoided in formal writing.

folks. *Folks* is informal for "one's family; one's relatives." In academic writing, use a more formal expression than *folks*.

fun. When used as an adjective, *fun* is colloquial; it should be avoided in formal writing.

further, farther. See *farther, further*.

get. *Get* is a common verb with many slang and colloquial uses. Avoid the following uses of *get*: "to become"; "to obtain revenge"; "to annoy"; "to elicit an emotional response."

good, well. *Good* is an adjective. *Well* is nearly always an adverb. (See page 27.)

hanged, hung. *Hanged* is the past tense and past participle of *hang*, which means "to execute." *Hung* is the past tense and past participle of *hang*, which means "to fasten or be fastened to something."

hardly. Avoid double negative expressions such as *not hardly* or *can't hardly*. (See pages 29–30.)

has got, have got. Avoid using *have got* or *has got* when *have* or *has* alone communicate the intended meaning.

he. Do not use only *he* when the complete meaning is "he or she." In modern usage, this is not inclusive. See pages 11 and 53–55 for alternative constructions.

he/she, his/her. Use *he or she*, or *his or her* in formal writing. See pages 10–11 and 52–54 for alternative constructions.

hisself. Non-standard for *himself*.

hopefully. *Hopefully* is an adverb meaning "in a hopeful manner." *Hopefully* can modify a verb, an adjective, or another adverb. In formal writing, do not use *hopefully* as a sentence modifier with the meaning "I hope."

hung, hanged. See *hanged, hung*.

i.e. The abbreviation *i.e.* stands for the Latin *id est*, which in English means "that is." In formal writing, use the English equivalent, *that is*.

if, whether. *If* is used to express conditions. Use *whether* to express alternatives.

illicit, elicit. See *elicit, illicit*.

illusion, allusion. See *allusion, illusion*.

immanent, imminent, eminent. See *eminent, immanent, imminent*.

immigrate to, emigrate from. See *emigrate from, immigrate to*.

immoral, amoral. See *amoral, immoral*.

implement. As a verb, *implement* means "to carry out." It is often unnecessary and pretentious.

implicit, explicit. See *explicit, implicit*.

imply, infer. *Imply* means to "express indirectly." *Infer* means "to conclude by reasoning."

in, into. *In* generally indicates a location or condition. *Into* indicates a direction, a movement, or a change in condition.

individual. *Individual* is sometimes used as a pretentious substitute for *person*.

ingenious, ingenuous. *Ingenious* means "clever" or "skillful." *Ingenuous* means "frank" and "simple."

in regards to. *In regards to* confuses two phrases: *in regard to* and *as regards*. Use either one of these alternatives to *in regards to*.

irregardless. *Irregardless* is non-standard English. Use *regardless* instead.

irritate, aggravate. See *aggravate, irritate*.

is when, is where Do not use *when* or *where* following *is* in definitions.

it is. *It is* becomes non-standard when used to mean "there is."

its, it's. *Its* is a possessive pronoun. *It's* is a contraction for *it is*.

kind, kinds. *Kind* is singular and should not be treated as a plural. *Kinds* is plural.

kind of, sort of. *Kind of* and *sort of* are colloquial expressions meaning "rather" or "somewhat." Do not use these colloquialisms in formal writing.

lay, lie. See *lie, lay*.

lead, led. *Lead* is a soft heavy metal. *Led* is the past tense of the verb *lead*.

learn, teach. *Learn* means "to gain knowledge of or a skill by instruction, study, or experience." *Teach* means "to impart knowledge or a skill."

leave, let. *Leave* means "to go away." *Let* means "to allow or permit." Do not use *leave* with the non-standard meaning "to permit."

led, lead. See *lead, led*.

less, fewer. See *fewer, less*.

liable. *Liable* means "legally responsible." Avoid using it to mean "likely."

licence, license. *Licence* is a noun meaning "legal permission to do something." *License* is a verb meaning "to permit or authorize."

lie, lay. *Lie* means "to recline." It is an intransitive verb, which means it does not take a direct object. The principal forms of the verb are *lie*, *lay*, and *lain*. *Lay* means "to put" or "to place." It is a transitive verb, which means it requires a direct object. The principal parts of the verb are *lay*, *laid*, and *lain*.

like, as. *Like* is a preposition, and it should be followed by a noun or a noun phrase. As is a subordinating conjunction and should be used to introduce a dependent clause.

loose, lose. *Loose* is an adjective meaning "not firmly fastened." *Lose* is a verb meaning "to misplace" or "to be defeated."

lots, lots of. *Lots* and *lots of* are colloquial substitutes for *many, much,* and *a great deal.* They should not be used in formal writing.

male, female. See *female, male.*

mankind. *Mankind* is not an inclusive term, as it excludes women. Avoid it in favour of terms such as *humans, humanity, the human race,* or *humankind.*

may, can. See *can, may.*

may of, might of. *May of* and *might of* are non-standard English for *may have* and *might have.*

maybe, may be. *Maybe* is an adverb meaning "perhaps." *May be* is a verb phrase.

media, medium. *Media* is the plural of *medium.*

moral, morale. *Moral* is a noun meaning "an ethical conclusion." *Morale* means "the attitude as regards courage, confidence, and enthusiasm."

most. When used to mean "almost," *most* is colloquial. This usage should be avoided in formal writing.

must of. See *may of, might of.*

myself. *Myself* is a reflexive pronoun. *Myself* can also be an intensive pronoun. Do not use *myself* in place of *I* or *me.*

neither. *Neither* is most often singular. (See pages 10 and 22.)

none. *None* is usually singular. (See pages 10 and 22.)

nowheres. *Nowheres* is non-standard English for *nowhere.*

number, amount. See *amount, number.*

of. *Of* is a preposition. Do not use it in place of the verb *have* after *could, should, would, may, must,* and *might.*

off of. Omit *of* from the expression as *off* is sufficient.

OK, O.K., okay. All three forms are acceptable in informal writing and speech. However, avoid these colloquial expressions in formal writing and speech.

parameters. *Parameter* is a mathematical term that means "a quantity that is constant in a particular calculation or case but varies in other cases." It is sometimes used as jargon to mean any limiting or defining element or feature. Avoid such jargon and use precise English instead.

passed, past. *Passed* is the past tense of the verb *pass,* which means "to go by." *Past* commonly means "gone by; ended." Never use *past* as a verb.

people, persons. Use *people* to refer to a group of individuals who are anonymous and uncounted. Generally, use *persons* or *people* when referring to a countable number of individuals.

percent, per cent, percentage. Always use *percent* (also spelled *per cent*) with specific numbers. *Percentage* means "part of" or "portion," and it is used when no number is provided.

phenomenon, phenomena. *Phenomenon* means "a fact, event or circumstance that can be observed." *Phenomena* is the plural of *phenomenon*.

plus. *Plus* is a non-standard substitute for *and*. Do not use *plus* to join independent clauses.

p.m. See *a.m., p.m., A.M., P.M.*

practice, practise. *Practice* is a noun meaning "an action done several times over to gain a skill." *Practise* is a verb meaning "to do something again and again in order to learn it." In American spelling, both the noun and verb are spelled *practice*.

precede, proceed. *Precede* means "to go or come before." *Proceed* means "to go on after having stopped" or "to move forward."

principal, principle. The noun *principal* means "a chief person" or "a sum of money that has been borrowed or invested." The noun *principle* means "a fact or belief on which other ideas are based." Note too that there is an adjective form, *principal*, meaning "main."

proceed, precede. See *precede, proceed*.

quote, quotation. *Quote* is a verb meaning "to repeat the exact words of." *Quotation* is a noun meaning "a passage quoted." Do not use *quote* as a shortened form of *quotation*.

raise, rise. *Raise* means "to move to a higher level; to elevate." It is a transitive verb, which means it requires a direct object. *Rise* means "to go up." It is an intransitive verb, which means it does not require a direct object.

real, really. *Real* is an adjective. Occasionally, in informal speech and writing, it is used as an adverb, but this usage should be avoided in formal writing. *Really* is an adverb. (See page 27.) In informal writing and speech, *real* and *really* are used as intensifiers to mean "extremely" or "very"; such usage should be avoided in formal writing and speech.

reason is because. *Reason is because* is a redundant expression. Use *reason is that* instead.

reason why. *Reason why* is a redundant expression. In its place use either *reason* or *why*.

regretfully, regrettably. *Regretfully* means "full of regret." It describes a person's attitude of regret. *Regrettably* means that circumstances are regrettable.

relation, relationship. *Relation* is used to describe the association between two or more things. *Relationship* is used to describe the association or connection between people.

respectfully, respectively. *Respectfully* is an adverb meaning "showing or marked by proper respect." *Respectively* is an adverb meaning "singly in the order designated or mentioned."

rise, raise. See *raise, rise*.

sensual, sensuous. *Sensual* is an adjective meaning "relating to gratification of the physical senses." *Sensuous* is an adjective meaning "pleasing to the senses." *Sensuous* is always favourable and often applies to the appreciation of nature, art, or music.

set, sit. *Set* means "to set in place, position, or put down." It is a transitive verb, requiring a direct object, and its principal parts are *set, set, set*. *Sit* means "to be seated." It is an intransitive verb, not requiring a direct object, and its principal parts are *sit, sat, sat*. *Set* is sometimes a non-standard substitute for *sit*. Avoid this usage in formal writing.

shall, will. *Shall* was once used with the first-person singular and plural as the helping verb with future-tense verbs. In modern usage *will* has replaced *shall*. The word *shall* is still often used in polite questions and legal documents.

she/he, her/his. See *he/she, his/her*.

should of. *Should of* is non-standard for *should have*.

since. *Since* should mainly be used in situations describing time. Do not use *since* as a substitute for *because* if there is any chance of confusion.

sit, set. See *set, sit*.

site, cite. See *cite, site*.

somebody, someone. *Somebody* and *someone* are singular. (See pages 10 and 22.)

something. *Something* is singular. (See pages 10 and 22.)

sometime, some time, sometimes. *Sometime* is an adverb meaning "at an indefinite or unstated time." In *some time* the adjective *some* modifies the noun *time*. *Sometimes* is an adverb meaning "at times; now and then."

sort of, kind of. See *kind of, sort of*.

stationary, stationery. *Stationary* means "not moving." *Stationery* refers to paper and other writing products.

suppose to, use to. See *use to, suppose to*.

sure and. *Sure and* is non-standard. Instead, use *sure to*.

take, bring. See *bring, take*.

teach, learn. See *learn, teach*.

than, then. *Than* is a conjunction used to make comparisons. *Then* is an adverb used to indicate past or future time.

that, which. Most writers use *that* for restrictive clauses and *which* for non-restrictive clauses. (See page 66.)

that, who. See *who, which, that.*

theirselves. *Theirselves* is non-standard English for *themselves.*

them. *Them* is non-standard when it is used in place of *those.*

then, than. See *than, then.*

there, their, they're. *There* is an adverb meaning "at or in that place." *There* can also be an expletive, a phrase at the beginning of a clause. *Their* is a possessive pronoun. *They're* is a contraction for *they are.*

this kind. See *kind, kinds.*

thru. *Thru* is a colloquial spelling of *through.* Do not use *thru* in formal academic or business writing.

to, too, two. *To* is a preposition. *Too* is an adverb. *Two* is a number.

toward, towards. Both versions are acceptable; however, *toward* is preferred in Canadian English.

try and. *Try and* is non-standard English. Instead use *try to.*

ultimately, eventually. See *eventually, ultimately.*

uninterested, disinterested. See *disinterested, uninterested.*

unique. Like *straight, round,* and *complete, unique* is an absolute. There are no degrees of uniqueness. Especially in formal writing, avoid expressions such as *more unique* and *most unique.*
(See page 29.)

usage, use. *Usage* refers to conventions, most often of language. *Use* means "to employ." Do not substitute *usage* when *use* is required.

use to, suppose to. *Use to* and *suppose to* are non-standard for *used to* and *supposed to.*

utilize. *Utilize* means "to put to use." Often *use* can be substituted, as *utilize* makes writing sound pretentious.

wait for, wait on. *Wait for* means "to await." *Wait on* means "to serve." It should not be used as substitute for *wait for.*

ways. *Ways* is colloquial in usage when designating distance.

weather, whether. *Weather* is a noun describing "the state of the atmosphere at a given time and place." *Whether* is a conjunction that signals a choice between or among alternatives.

well, good. See *good, well.*

where. *Where* is non-standard in usage when it is substituted for *that* as a subordinate conjunction.

whether, if. See *if, whether.*

which. See *that, which* and *who, which, that.*

while. Do not use *while* as a substitute for "although" or "whereas" if such usage might create ambiguity.

who, which, that. Use *who* not *which* to refer to persons. Usually, *that* is used to refer to things. However, *that* may be used to refer to a class or group of people.

who, whom. *Who* is used for subjects and subject complements. *Whom* is used for objects. (See page 18.)

who's, whose. *Who's* is a contraction for *who is*. *Whose* is a possessive pronoun.

will, shall. See *shall, will*.

would of. *Would of* is non-standard English for *would have*.

you. Avoid using *you* in an indefinite sentence to mean "anyone." (See page 14.)

your, you're. *Your* is a possessive pronoun. *You're* is a contraction for *you are*.

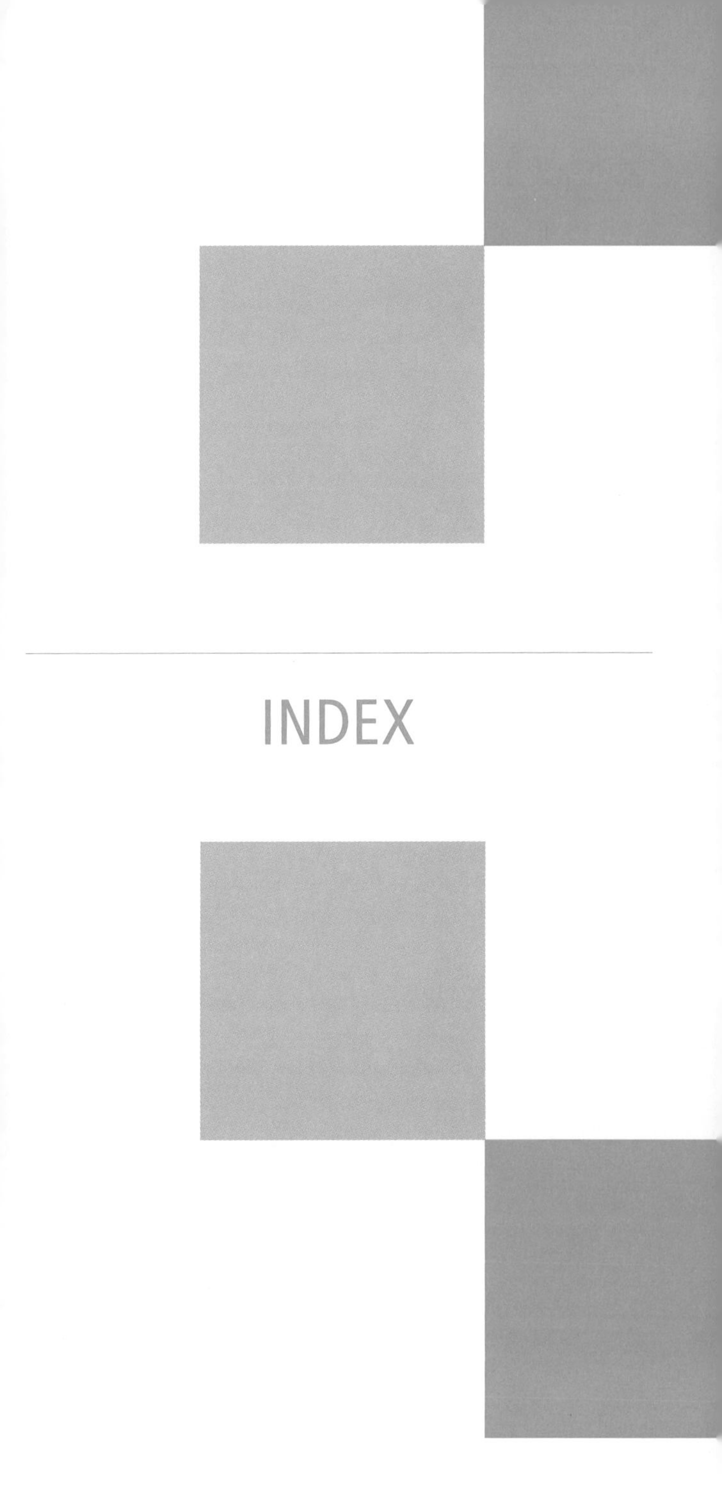

INDEX

$, 95

a, an, 146
Abbreviations, 83, 94–98
Absolute concepts, 29
Absolute phrases, 78
Abstract noun, 56
accept, except, 146
Active voice, 36, 47, 57–59
A.D., 95
adapt, adopt, 146
Address, 69–70
Adjective, 26–30
Adverb, 26–30
Adverbial clause, 64
adverse, averse, 146
advice, advise, 146
affect, effect, 147
aggravate, irritate, 147
Agreement
  pronoun–antecedent, 10–12
  subject–verb, 19–26 (*see also* Subject–verb agreement)
agree to, agree with, 147
ain't, 147
all ready, already, 147
all right, alright, 147
allude, elude, 147
allusion, illusion, delusion, 147
alot, a lot, 147
altogether, all together, 147
a.m., A.M., 95, 147
among, between, 148
amount, number, 147
and ... etc., 147
and/or, 148
ante-, anti-, 148
Antecedent, 10
anxious, eager, 148
anyone, any one, 148
anyplace, 148
anyways, anywheres, 148
APA style of documentation, 123–33
  books, 125–26
  conference proceedings published in a book, 129
  dissertation abstract, 129
  electronic sources, 125, 127–29
  film, videotape, DVD, 129
  format, 129
  government document, 129
  in-text citations, 123–25
  periodicals, 126–27
  References list, 125–31
  sample paper, 130–33
Apostrophe, 74–77
Appositive, 16, 38
as, 17, 41, 148
averse, adverse, 148
awhile, a while, 148
Awkwardly placed modifier, 31–32

bad, badly, 148
barely, 30
B.C., 95
B.C.E., 95
be, 20
being as, being that, 148
beside, besides, 148
between, among, 148
Bible, 104, 110
Bibliographic notes, 118
Brackets, 86–87
bring, take, 148
burst, bursted, 148
bust, busted, 148

can, may, 148
capital, capitol, 148
Capitalization, 90–94
Case, 14–18
CBE style of documentation, 139, 143–44
C.E., 95
censor, censure, 148
Chicago Manual of Style, 134
Chicago style of documentation, 134–42
  books, 135–37
  electronic sources, 138–39
  endnotes, 134–35
  periodicals, 137–38
  sample essay, 140–42
Citations. *See* Documentation
Citation-sequence system, 139
cite, site, 148
Cliché, 60–61
climactic, climatic, 148
coarse, course, 148
Collective noun, 11–12, 23–24
Colon, 73–74
Colourless verbs, 46–47
Comma, 63–71
  absolute phrases, 78
  address, 69–70
  clarifying writer's intention, 71
  concluding adverb clauses, 66–67
  coordinate adjectives, 65
  cumulative adjectives, 65–66
  date, 69
  echoing words, 70
  expressions of contrast, 68
  he said, etc., 69
  independent clauses with coordinating conjunction, 64
  introductory elements, 64–65
  items in series, 65
  mild interjection, 69
  nouns of direct address, 69
  numbers, 70
  omitted words, 70
  parenthetical expressions, 68
  restrictive/non-restrictive elements, 66
  title, 70
  transitional expressions, 67–68
  yes, no, 69
Command, 83
Comma splice, 6–10
Common noun, 90–91
Comparatives, 28–29
compare to, compare with, 148
Comparisons, 17, 41
complement, compliment, 148
Compound antecedent, 12
Compound object, 15–16
Compound predicate, 5
Compound subject, 15–16, 21
Conciseness (wordiness), 44–47
Concluding adverb clauses, 66–67
Concrete noun, 56

Conjunction
  coordinating, 7, 40
  correlative, 40
Conjunctive adverb, 7, 71
Connotation, 55–56
consensus of opinion, 148
conscience, conscious, 148
contact, 148
Content notes, 118
continual, continuous, 148
Contractions, 76
Coordinate adjectives, 65
Coordinating conjunction, 7, 40
Copyright page, 107
Correlative conjunction, 40
could care less, 150
could of, 150
council, counsel, 150
criteria, criterion, 150
Cumulative adjectives, 65–66

Dangling modifier, 32–33
Dash, 85–86
data, datum, 150
Date, 69
delusion, illusion, allusion, 147
Denotative meaning, 55
Diction and audience, 47–61
  active verbs, 57–59
  cliché, 60–61
  connotation, 55–56
  euphemism, 50
  figures of speech, 61
  idiom, 59–60
  jargon, 48–49
  levels of formality, 52–53
  misused words, 59
  non-standard English, 51–52
  nonsexist language, 53–55
  nouns, 56–57
  pretentious language, 49–50
  regional expression, 51
  slang, 50–51
different from, different than, 150
differ from, differ with, 150
Direct object, 15
Direct question, 36, 83
Direct quotation, 36, 77–78
discreet, discrete, 150
disinterested, uninterested, 150
do, 20
Documentation
  APA style, 123–33
  CBE style, 139, 143–44
  Chicago Manual of Style, 134–42
  MLA style, 100–122
$, 95
don't, 150
Double comparatives/
 superlatives, 29
Double negatives, 29–30
due to, 150

each, 150
eager, anxious, 148
Echoing words, 70
effect, affect, 147
e.g., 150
either, 150
Electronic sources
  APA style, 125, 127–29
  CBE style, 144
  Chicago Manual of Style, 138–39
  MLA style, 105–6, 113–16
elicit, illicit, 150
Ellipsis mark (...), 87
Elliptical clause, 33
elude, allude, 147
emigrate from, immigrate to, 151
eminent, immanent, imminent, 151
Empty/inflated phrases, 45–46
Endnote, 118, 119, 134
enthused, enthusiastic, 151
-ess, 151
etc., 151
Euphemism, 50
eventually, ultimately, 151
everybody, everyone, 151
everyone, every one, 151
except, accept, 146
except for the fact that, 151
Exclamation point, 84
Expletive construction, 24, 47
explicit, implicit, 151
Expressions of contrast, 68

farther, further, 151
Faulty apposition, 38
Faulty parallelism, 39
Faulty predication, 38
female, male, 151
fewer, less, 151
Figures of speech, 61
finalize, 151
First-person point of view, 34
flunk, 151
folks, 152
Footnote, 118, 119, 134
for example, 5
for instance, 5
Formality (wording), 52–53
Formal writing, 52
Four-digit numbers, 70
Fragments, 2–6. *See also* Sentence fragments
fun, 152
Fused sentence, 6–10

Gender neutral language, 53–55
General abstract nouns, 56
General noun, 56
Generic noun, 11
Gerund, 18
Gerund phrase, 32
get, 152
Glossary of usage, 146–58
good, well, 152
Grammar, 1–41
  adjectives/adverbs, 26–30
  comma splices/fused sentences, 6–10
  mixed constructions, 37–39
  modifiers, 30–33
  parallelism, 39–41
  pronouns, 10–19
  sentence fragments, 2–6
  shifts, 33–37
  subject–verb agreement, 19–26

hanged, hung, 152
hardly, 30, 152
has got, have got, 152
have, 20
he, 152
he said, 69
he/she, his/her, 152
hisself, 152
hopefully, 152

Idiom, 59–60
i.e., 152
if, whether, 152
illicit, elicit, 150
Illogical connection, 38
illusion, allusion, delusion, 147
immanent, imminent, eminent, 151
immigrate to, emigrate from, 151
Imperative mood, 35
implement, 152
implicit, explicit, 151
Implied antecedent, 13
imply, infer, 152
in, into, 153
Indefinite pronoun, 10, 22–23, 76
Independent clause, 3, 6, 71
Indicative mood, 35
Indirect object, 15
Indirect question, 36, 83
Indirect quotation, 36, 77
individual, 153
Infinitive, 17, 32
Infinitive phrase, 32
Inflated phrase, 45–46
Information notes (MLA), 118–19
ingenious, ingenuous, 153
in regards to, 153
Interjection, 69
Interrogative pronoun, 18
In-text citations
  APA style, 123–25
  CBE style, 143
  MLA style, 100–106
  See also Documentation
Introducing quoted material, 81–82
Introductory adverbial clause, 64
Introductory elements, 64–65
Inverting sentence order, 24
irregardless, 153
irritate, aggravate, 147
is when, is where, 38, 153
Items in series. *See* Series
it is, 47, 153
its, it's, 153

Jargon, 48–49

kind, kinds, 153
kind of, sort of, 153

Latin abbreviations, 96
lead, led, 153
learn, teach, 153
leave, let, 153
less, fewer, 151
Levels of formality, 52–53
liable, 153
licence, license, 153
lie, lay, 153
like, as, 153
Linking verb, 27
Lists
  colon, 73
  fragments, 6
  See also Series
Longer introductory phrases, 65
loose, lose, 154
lots, lots of, 154

Main clause, 6
male, female, 151
mankind, 154
may, can, 148
maybe, may be, 154
may of, might of, 154
Mechanics
  abbreviations, 94–98
  capitalization, 90–94
media, medium, 154
Metaphor, 61
Metric abbreviations, 97
Mild command, 83
Mild interjection, 69
Misplaced modifier, 30, 31
Misused words, 59
Mixed constructions, 37–39
Mixed grammar, 37–38
Mixed metaphor, 61
MLA Handbook for Writers of Research Papers, 100, 119
MLA Style Manual and Guide to Scholarly Publishing, 119
MLA style of documentation, 100–122
  Bible, 104, 110
  books, 106–11
  dissertation, 117
  electronic sources, 105–6, 113–16
  film, videotape, DVD, 117–18
  format, 120
  government publications, 116
  information notes, 118–19
  interview, 117
  in-text citations, 100–106
  lecture (public address), 117
  pamphlet, 116–17
  periodicals, 111–12
  radio, TV program, 118
  sample paper, 120–22
  sound recording, 118
  Works Cited, 106–18
Modifier
  awkwardly placed, 31–32
  dangling, 32–33
  defined, 30
  misplaced, 30, 31
  split infinitive, 32
Mood, 35–36
Mood shift, 36
moral, morale, 154
most, 154
must of, 154
myself, 154

Name–year system, 139
neither, 22–23, 154
no, 69
no., 95
none, 22–23, 154

Non-restrictive elements, 66
Nonsexist language, 53–55
Non-standard English, 51–52
nor, 21–22
Noun, 56–57
abstract, 56
collective, 11–12, 23–24
common, 90–91
concrete, 56
general, 56
generic, 11
possessive, 74–75
proper, 90–91
specific, 56
Nouns of direct address, 69
nowheres, 154
number, 23
number, amount, 147
Numbers, 70

Objective case, 14, 15–16
Object of a preposition, 15
of, 154
off of, 154
OK, O.K., okay, 154
Omitted words, 70
one of the, 25
only one of the, 25
or, 21–22

Parallelism, 39–41
parameters, 154
Parentheses, 86
Parenthetical expressions, 68
Participial phrase, 32
passed, past, 154
Passive voice, 36, 47, 57–59
people, persons, 154
percent, per cent, percentage, 155
Period, 82–84
Personification, 61
phenomenon, phenomena, 155
Phrase, 4, 32
Phrase fragments, 4
Plurals, 76–77
plus, 155
p.m., P.M., 95, 147
Poetry
citations, 104
ellipsis, 87–88
quotation marks, 78
slash, 88
Possessive case, 14, 18
Possessive indefinite pronouns, 76
Possessive nouns, 74–75
practice, practise, 155
precede, proceed, 155
Predicate, 5
Present tense, 19–20
Pretentious language, 49–50
principal, principle, 155
Pronoun, 10–19
antecedents, and, 10–12
case, 14–18
defined, 10
indefinite, 10, 22–23, 76
interrogative, 18
reference, 12–14
reflexive, 16
relative, 25
who, whom, 18–19
Pronoun–antecedent agreement, 10–12
Pronoun case, 14–18
Pronoun reference, 12–14
Proper names, 91–92, 94
Proper noun, 90–91
Publication information, 107–8
Punctuation, 63–88
apostrophe, 74–77
brackets, 86–87
colon, 73–74
comma, 63–71 (*see also* Comma)
dash, 85–86
ellipsis mark, 87
exclamation point, 84
parentheses, 86
period, 82–84
question mark, 84
quotation marks, 77–82 (*see also* Quotations)
semicolon, 71–73
slash, 88

Question mark, 84
Quotations, 77–82
commas/periods, 80
direct, 77–78
incorrect uses, 82
introducing quoted material, 81–82
long quotations, 78–79
question marks/exclamation points, 80–81
quotations with quotations, 79
semicolons/colons, 80
titles, 79
words as words, 79
Quotations within quotations, 79
quote, quotation, 155

raise, rise, 155
real, really, 155
reason ... is because, 39, 155
reason why, 155
Reducing clauses/phrases, 47
Redundancy, 44
References list (APA style), 125–31
Reflexive pronoun, 16
Regional expressions, 51
regretfully, regrettably, 155
relation, relationship, 155
Relative pronouns, 25
respectfully, respectively, 156
Restrictive/non-restrictive elements, 66
Run-on sentence, 6–10

scarcely, 30
Scientific Style and Format: The CBE Manual for Authors, Editors, and Publishers, 139
Second-person point of view, 34
Semicolon, 71–73
sensual, sensuous, 156
Sentence, 2
Sentence fragments
acceptable fragments, 6
compound predicate, 5
defined, 2
examples, 5
lists, 6

phrase fragments, 4
subordinate clause, 3–4
testing for, 2–3
Series
comma, 65
parallelism, 39–40
semicolon, 72
set, sit, 156
Sexist language, 53–55
shall, will, 156
she said, 69
Shifts, 33–37
defined, 33
indirect/direct questions/quotations, 36–37
point of view, 34–35
verb mood/voice, 35–36
verb tense, 35
should of, 156
Simile, 61
Simplifying structure, 46–47
since, 156
site, cite, 148
Slang, 50–51
Slash, 88
somebody, someone, 156
something, 156
sometime, some time, sometimes, 156
sort of, kind of, 153
Specific noun, 56
Split infinitive, 32
Standard English, 52
stationary, stationery, 156
Stereotyping, 54
Strengthening the verb, 46
Style
diction and audience, 47–61 (*see also* Diction and audience)
wordiness, 44–47
Subject complement, 24, 27
Subjective case, 14, 15
Subject–verb agreement, 19–26
collective nouns, 23–24
indefinite pronoun, 22–23
plural form, singular meaning, 25
relative pronouns, 25
subject after verb, 24
subject complement, 24
subjects with *and*, 21
subjects with *or* or *nor*, 21
title and words as words, 26
work between subject and verb, 20–21
Subjunctive mood, 35
Subordinate clause, 3–4
such as, 5
Superlatives, 28–29
sure and, 156

take, bring, 148
teach, learn, 153
Tense shift, 35
than, 17, 41
than, then, 156
that, 25
that, which, 157
that, who, which, 158
theirselves, 157
them, 157
there, their, they're, 157
there is, 47
Third-person point of view, 34
this kind, 157
thru, 157
Title
capitalization, 91–92
comma, 70
quotation mark, 79
subject–verb agreement, 26
to, too, two, 157
toward, towards, 157
Transitional expressions, 67–68, 71–72
Transitional phrases, 72
try and, 157

ultimately, eventually, 151
Unidiomatic expressions, 60
uninterested, disinterested, 150
unique, 157
Unit of measurement, 24
Unnecessary repetition of words, 45
usage, use, 157
Usage (glossary of usage), 146–58
use to, suppose to, 157
utilize, 157

Verb mood/voice, 35–36
Verb tense, 35
Voice, 36

wait for, wait on, 157
ways, 157
weather, whether, 157
well, good, 152
where, 157
whether, if, 152
which, 25
which, that, 157
while, 157
who, 25
who, which, that, 158
who, whom, 18–19, 158
who's, whose, 158
will, shall, 156
Wordiness, 44–47
Wording. *See* Diction and audience
Words as words, 26, 79
Works Cited (MLA style), 106–18
would of, 158

yes, no, 69
you, 14
your, you're, 158